3.99

MACMI

MASTER GUIDES

GENERAL EDITOR: JAMES GIBSON

JANE AUSTEN	*Emma* Norman Page
	Sense and Sensibility Judy Simons
	Persuasion Judy Simons
	Pride and Prejudice Raymond Wilson
	Mansfield Park Richard Wirdnam
SAMUEL BECKETT	*Waiting for Godot* Jennifer Birkett
WILLIAM BLAKE	*Songs of Innocence and Songs of Experience* Alan Tomlinson
ROBERT BOLT	*A Man for All Seasons* Leonard Smith
CHARLOTTE BRONTË	*Jane Eyre* Robert Miles
EMILY BRONTË	*Wuthering Heights* Hilda D. Spear
JOHN BUNYAN	*The Pilgrim's Progress* Beatrice Batson
GEOFFREY CHAUCER	*The Miller's Tale* Michael Alexander
	The Pardoner's Tale Geoffrey Lester
	The Wife of Bath's Tale Nicholas Marsh
	The Knight's Tale Anne Samson
	The Prologue to the Canterbury Tales Nigel Thomas and Richard Swan
JOSEPH CONRAD	*The Secret Agent* Andrew Mayne
CHARLES DICKENS	*Bleak House* Dennis Butts
	Great Expectations Dennis Butts
	Hard Times Norman Page
GEORGE ELIOT	*Middlemarch* Graham Handley
	Silas Marner Graham Handley
	The Mill on the Floss Helen Wheeler
T. S. ELIOT	*Selected Poems* Andrew Swarbrick
HENRY FIELDING	*Joseph Andrews* Trevor Johnson
E. M. FORSTER	*A Passage to India* Hilda D. Spear
	Howards End Ian Milligan
WILLIAM GOLDING	*The Spire* Rosemary Sumner
	Lord of the Flies Raymond Wilson
OLIVER GOLDSMITH	*She Stoops to Conquer* Paul Ranger
THOMAS HARDY	*The Mayor of Casterbridge* Ray Evans
	Tess of the d'Urbervilles James Gibson
	Far from the Madding Crowd Colin Temblett-Wood
BEN JONSON	*Volpone* Michael Stout
JOHN KEATS	*Selected Poems* John Garrett
RUDYARD KIPLING	*Kim* Leonée Ormond
PHILIP LARKIN	*The Whitsun Weddings* and *The Less Deceived* Andrew Swarbrick
D.H. LAWRENCE	*Sons and Lovers* R. P. Draper

MACMILLAN MASTER GUIDES

MACMILLAN MASTER GUIDES

MACBETH

BY WILLIAM SHAKESPEARE

DAVID ELLOWAY

MACMILLAN

First published 1985 by
MACMILLAN PRESS LTD
Houndmills, Basingstoke, Hampshire RG21 6XS
and London
Companies and representatives
throughout the world

ISBN 0–333–37203–4

A catalogue record for this book is available
from the British Library.

18 17 16 15 14 13 12 11 10
04 03 02 01 00 99 98 97 96

Printed in Hong Kong

CONTENTS

GENERAL EDITOR'S PREFACE

The aim of the Macmillan Master Guides is to help you to appreciate the book you are studying by providing information about it and by suggesting ways of reading and thinking about it which will lead to a fuller understanding. The section on the writer's life and background has been designed to illustrate those aspects of the writer's life which have influenced the work, and to place it in its personal and literary context. The summaries and critical commentary are of special importance in that each brief summary of the action is followed by an examination of the significant critical points. The space which might have been given to repetitive explanatory notes has been devoted to a detailed analysis of the kind of passage which might confront you in an examination. Literary criticism is concerned with both the broader aspects of the work being studied and with its detail. The ideas which meet us in reading a great work of literature, and their relevance to us today, are an essential part of our study, and our Guides look at the thought of their subject in some detail. But just as essential is the craft with which the writer has constructed his work of art, and this is considered under several technical headings – characterisation, language, style and stagecraft.

The authors of these Guides are all teachers and writers of wide experience, and they have chosen to write about books they admire and know well in the belief that they can communicate their admiration to you. But you yourself must read and know intimately the book you are studying. No one can do that for you. You should see this book as a lamppost. Use it to shed light, not to lean against. If you know your text and know what it is saying about life, and how it says it, then you will enjoy it, and there is no better way of passing an examination in literature.

JAMES GIBSON

AN INTRODUCTION TO THE STUDY OF SHAKESPEARE'S PLAYS

A play as a work of art exists to the full only when performed. It must hold the audience's attention throughout the performance, and, unlike a novel, it can't be put down and taken up again. It is important to experience the play as if you are seeing it on the stage for the first time, and you should begin by reading it straight through. Shakespeare builds a play in dramatic units which may be divided into smaller subdivisions, or episodes, marked off by exits and entrances and lasting as long as the same actors are on the stage. Study it unit by unit.

The first unit provides the exposition which is designed to put the audience into the picture. In the second unit we see the forward movement of the play as one situation changes into another. The last unit in a tragedy or a tragical play will bring the catastrophe and in comedy – and some of the history plays – an unravelling of the complications, what is called a *dénouement*.

The onward movement of the play from start to finish is its progressive structure. We see the chain of cause and effect (the plot) and the progressive revelation and development of character. The people, their characters and their motives drive the plot forward in a series of scenes which are carefully planned to give variety of pace and excitement. We notice fast-moving and slower-moving episodes, tension mounting and slackening, and alternate fear and hope for the characters we favour. Full-stage scenes, such as stately councils and processions or turbulent mobs, contrast with scenes of small groups or even single speakers. Each of the scenes presents a deed or event which changes the situation. In performance, entrances and exits and stage actions are physical facts, with more impact than on the page. That impact Shakespeare relied upon, and we must restore it by an effort of the imagination.

Shakespeare's language is just as diverse. Quickfire dialogue is followed by long speeches, and verse changes to prose. There is a wide range of speech – formal, colloquial, dialect, 'Mummerset' and the broken English of foreigners, for example. Songs, instrumental music, and the noise of battle, revelry and tempest, all extend the range of dramatic expression. The dramatic use of language is enhanced by skilful stagecraft, by costumes, by properties such as beds, swords and Yorick's skull, by such stage business as kneeling, embracing and giving money, and by use of such features of the stage structure as the balcony and the trapdoor.

By these means Shakespeare's people are brought vividly to life and cleverly individualised. But though they have much to tell us about human nature, we must never forget that they are characters in a play, not in real life. And remember, they exist to enact the play, not the play to portray *them.*

Shakespeare groups his characters so that they form a pattern, and it is useful to draw a diagram showing this. Sometimes a linking character has dealings with each group. The pattern of persons belongs to the symmetric structure of the play, and its dramatic unity is reinforced and enriched by a pattern of resemblances and contrasts; for instance, between characters, scenes, recurrent kinds of imagery, and words. It is not enough just to notice a feature that belongs to the symmetric structure, you should ask what its relevance is to the play as a whole and to the play's ideas.

These ideas and the dramatising of them in a central theme, or several related to each other, are a principal source of the dramatic unity. In order to see what themes are present and important, look, as before, for pattern. Observe the place in it of the leading character. In tragedy this will be the protagonist, in comedy heroes and heroines, together with those in conflict or contrast with them. In *I Henry IV*, Prince Hal is being educated for kingship and has a correct estimate of honour, while Falstaff despises honour, and Hotspur makes an idol of it. Pick out the episodes of great intensity as, for example, in *King Lear* where the theme of spiritual blindness is objectified in the blinding of Gloucester, and, similarly, note the emphases given by dramatic poetry as in Prospero's 'Our revels now are ended. . .' or unforgettable utterances such as Lear's 'Is there any cause in Nature that makes these hard hearts?' Striking stage-pictures such as that of Hamlet behind the King at prayer will point to leading themes, as will all the parallels and recurrences, including those of phrase and imagery. See whether, in the play you are studying, themes known to be favourites with Shakespeare are prominent, themes such as those of order and disorder, relationships disrupted by mistakes about identity, and appearance and reality. The latter were bound to fascinate Shakespeare whose theatrical art worked by means of illusions which pointed beyond the surface of actual life to underlying truths. In looking at themes beware of attempts to make the play fit some orthodoxy a critic believes in – Freudian perhaps, or Marxist, or dogmatic Christian theology – and remember that its ideas, though they often have a bearing on ours, are Elizabethan.

Some of Shakespeare's greatness lies in the good parts he wrote for the actors. In his demands upon them, and the opportunities he provided, he bore their professional skills in mind and made use of their physical prowess, relished by a public accustomed to judge fencing and wrestling as expertly as we today judge football and tennis. As a member of the professional group of players called the Chamberlain's Men he knew each actor he was writing for. To play his women he had highly-trained boys. As paired heroines they were often contrasted, short with tall, for example, or one vivacious and enterprising, the other more conventionally feminine.

Richard Burbage, the company's leading man, was famous as a great tragic actor, and he took leading roles in seven of Shakespeare's *tragedies*. Though each of the seven has its own distinctiveness, we shall find at the centre of all of them a tragic protagonist possessing tragic greatness, not just one 'tragic flaw' but a tragic vulnerability. He will have a character which makes him unfit to cope with the tragic situations confronting him, so that his tragic errors bring down upon him tragic suffering and finally a tragic catastrophe. Normally, both the suffering and the catastrophe are far worse than he can be said to deserve, and others are engulfed in them who deserve such a fate less or not at all. Tragic terror is aroused in us because, though exceptional, he is sufficiently near to normal humankind for his fate to remind us of what can happen to human beings like ourselves, and because we see in it a combination of inexorable law and painful mystery. We recognise the principle of cause and effect where in a tragic world errors return upon those who make them, but we are also aware of the tragic disproportion between cause and effect. In a tragic world you may kick a stone and start an avalanche which will destroy you and others with you. Tragic pity is aroused in us by this disproportionate suffering, and also by all the kinds of suffering undergone by every character who has won our imaginative sympathy. Imaginative sympathy is wider than moral approval, and is felt even if suffering does seem a just and logical outcome. In addition to pity and terror we have a sense of tragic waste because catastrophe has affected so much that was great and fine. Yet we feel also a tragic exaltation. To our grief the men and women who represented those values have been destroyed, but the values themselves have been shown not to depend upon success, nor upon immunity from the worst of tragic suffering and disaster.

Comedies have been of two main kinds, or cross-bred from the two. In critical comedies the governing aim is to bring out the absurdity or irrationality of follies and abuses, and make us laugh at them. Shakespeare's comedies often do this, but most of them belong primarily to the other kind – romantic comedy. Part of the romantic appeal is to our liking for suspense; they are dramas of averted threat, beginning in trouble and ending in joy. They appeal to the romantic senses of adventure and of wonder, and to complain that they are improbable is silly because the improbability, the marvellousness, is part of the pleasure. They dramatise stories of romantic love, accompanied by love doctrine – ideas and ideals of love. But they are plays in two tones, they are comic as well as romantic. There is often something to laugh at even in the love stories of the nobility and gentry, and just as there is high comedy in such incidents as the cross-purposes of the young Athenians in the wood, and Rosalind as 'Ganymede' teasing Orlando, there is always broad comedy for characters of lower rank. Even where one of the sub-plots has no effect on the main plot, it may take up a topic from it and present it in a more comic way.

What is there in the play to make us laugh or smile? We can distinguish many kinds of comedy it may employ. *Language* can amuse by its wit, or by absurdity, as in Bottom's malapropisms. Feste's nonsense-phrases, so fatuously admired by Sir Andrew, are deliberate, while his catechising of Olivia is clown-routine. Ass-headed Bottom embraced by the Fairy Queen is a *comic spectacle* combining costume and stage-business. His wanting to play every part is *comedy of character*. Phebe disdaining Silvius and in love with 'Ganymede', or Malvolio treating Olivia as though she had written him a love-letter is *comedy of situation*; the situation is laughably different from what Phebe or Malvolio supposes. A comic let-down or anticlimax can be devastating, as we see when Aragon, sure that he deserves Portia, chooses the silver casket only to find the portrait not of her but of a 'blinking idiot'. By *slapstick, caricature* or sheer *ridiculousness of situation*, comedy can be exaggerated into farce, which Shakespeare knows how to use on occasion. At the opposite extreme, before he averts the threat, he can carry it to the brink of tragedy, but always under control.

Dramatic irony is the result of a character or the audience anticipating an outcome which, comically or tragically, turns out very differently. Sometimes *we* foresee that it will. The speaker never foresees how ironical, looking back, the words or expectations will appear. When she says, 'A little water clears us of this deed' Lady Macbeth has no prevision of her sleep-walking words, 'Will these hands ne'er be clean?' There is irony in the way in which in all Shakespeare's tragic plays except *Richard II* comedy is found in the very heart of the tragedy. The Porter scene in *Macbeth* comes straight after Duncan's murder. In *Hamlet* and *Antony and Cleopatra* comic episodes lead into the catastrophe: the rustic Countryman brings Cleopatra the means of death, and the satirised Osric departs with Hamlet's assent to the fatal fencing match. The Porter, the Countryman and Osric are not mere 'comic relief', they contrast with the tragedy in a way that adds something to it, and affects our response.

A sense of the comic and the tragic is common ground between Shakespeare and his audience. Understandings shared with the audience are necessary to all drama. They include conventions, i.e. assumptions, contrary to what factual realism would demand, which the audience silently agrees to accept. It is, after all, by a convention, what Coleridge called a 'willing suspension of disbelief', that an actor is accepted as Hamlet. We should let a play teach us the conventions it depends on. Shakespeare's conventions allow him to take a good many liberties, and he never troubles about inconsistencies that wouldn't trouble an audience. What matters to the dramatist is the effect he creates. So long as we are responding as he would wish, Shakespeare would not care whether we could say by what means he has made us do so. But to appreciate his skill, and get a fuller understanding of his play, we have to distinguish these means, and find terms to describe them.

If you approach the Shakespeare play you are studying bearing in mind what is said to you here, then you will respond to it more fully than before. Yet like all works of artistic genius, Shakespeare's can only be analysed so far. His drama and its poetry will always have about them something 'which into words no critic can digest'.

HAROLD BROOKS

ACKNOWLEDGEMENTS

Cover illustration: *The Weird Sisters*, School of Fuseli, courtesy of the Governors of the Royal Shakespeare Theatre. The drawing of the Globe Theatre is by courtesy of Alec Pearson.

NOTE. References to the play use the line numbering of the Macmillan Shakespeare edition of *Macbeth* but, as all references are clearly identified, this Study Guide may be used with any edition of the play.

1 LIFE AND BACKGROUND

1.1 LIFE

William Shakespeare was born in Stratford-upon-Avon in 1564. His father was a prosperous tradesman and occupied a number of important civic offices, but in the later 1570s his fortunes seem to have declined rapidly. In 1580 he was fined a considerable sum for some unknown offence and by 1592 he was failing to observe the legal requirement to attend church once a month for fear of being arrested for debt.

His son would almost certainly have been educated at the local grammar school, but there is no record of his early years until his marriage to Anne Hathaway in November 1582. It seems to have been a hasty marriage; a daughter, Susanna, was born six months later, followed by twins, Hamnet and Judith, in 1585. Within a few years of their birth Shakespeare had left Stratford for London. One can only speculate about the reasons for this move, but he must soon have begun his career both as actor and dramatist; before leaving Stratford he could have made contact with the companies of actors that regularly visited the town, and his introduction to the literary world may have been helped by a Stratford friend, Richard Field, who had been apprenticed to a London publisher in 1579 and opened his own shop in 1587. His earliest plays are generally dated 1589 or 1590, and by 1592 he was sufficiently well established for Robert Greene to warn his fellow university-educated dramatists against the competition from this upstart actor who presumed to write plays. By 1594 he was a member of the Lord Chamberlain's company, the most successful of the London theatre companies, led by the great tragic actor, Richard Burbage. They were frequently summoned to entertain the Queen, and when James I succeeded Elizabeth in 1603 they came under his personal patronage as the King's Men.

Shakespeare prospered in the theatre, becoming the most popular dramatist in the last decade of the century. He would have earned little as an actor or as a playwright, but he profited from sharing in the proceeds of the theatre itself; when the Chamberlain's Men moved to the newly built Globe Theatre in 1599 he had a tenth share in the enterprise. Meanwhile he had acquired his own noble patron, the Earl of Southampton, to whom he dedicated his two narrative poems and may have addressed many of the sonnets he wrote during these years. By 1596 the fortunes of his family were sufficiently restored for it to be granted a coat of arms, and in 1597 he bought New Place, one of the largest houses in Stratford.

He continued as a full member of the King's Men until at least 1611, the date usually ascribed to *The Tempest* – Shakespeare's plays can rarely be dated with complete certainty; the dates given here are those that seem most probable. This is the last play that can be attributed wholly to him and it is generally assumed that after its completion he lived in partial retirement at Stratford, although he subsequently wrote a large part, if not all, of *Henry VIII*. He died in 1616.

Shakespeare began by writing plays based on English history, concluding with *Henry V* in 1599. In the same decade he wrote most of his comedies, but only two tragedies, although several of the history plays are tragic in form. In 1599 he began the great series of tragedies with *Julius Caesar*. There followed the enigmatic psychological tragedy of *Hamlet*, the painfully intense domestic tragedy of *Othello* (1604), and his two darkest plays, *King Lear* (1605) and *Macbeth* (1606), the former an exploration of the extremes of human cruelty and suffering, the latter a concentrated study of the nature of evil. Thereafter the mood of his final three tragedies is less overwhelmingly bleak, and in his last years he turned to romances, plays in which situations as potentially distressing as those of the tragedies are resolved into mellow comedy by supernatural, or near-supernatural, means. He had not entirely given up comedy, but after *Twelfth Night* (1601) it lost much of the buoyancy and delight of the earlier plays, exploring the darker side of human nature with a moral intensity and a melancholy, often satirical, wit that matches the comic elements to be found in most of the tragedies, such as the episode of the Porter in *Macbeth*.

The change that came over Shakespeare's plays in the early years of the new century was part of a general change of theatrical fashion; as a whole, Jacobean drama is distinguished from Elizabethan by the predominance of darker tragedy and more realistic and satirical comedy. This has often been attributed to a growing mood of anxiety and disillusionment in the country. Economic conditions were worsening, there had been a series of disastrous harvests and a number of serious outbreaks of the plague. National pride and optimism had reached a peak with the defeat of the Spanish Armada in 1588, but since then the war had dragged on, draining the country's resources. There had been one further triumph, the sack of Cadiz in 1596, but the hero of that engagement, the gallant but immature and unstable Earl of Essex, ended his career abruptly with a rash attempt to seize power in 1601. His execution was widely lamented, and Shakespeare's patron, Southampton, was lucky to escape with imprisonment.

The threat of civil disorder was never far away during the sixteenth century, and as Elizabeth's long reign drew to a close uneasiness about what the future might hold was increased by the uncertainty as to who would succeed her. None of Henry VIII's children had produced a direct heir to the throne and, while James VI of Scotland was next in line, there were numerous other possible claimants – one of Essex's grievances was his suspicion that his enemies at court were advancing rival claims. The peaceful accession of James, as James I of England, put an end to these immediate anxieties, but Shakespeare certainly remembered them when he wrote *Macbeth* three years later.

1.2 THE POLITICAL BACKGROUND AND THE DOCTRINE OF ORDER

One of the earliest performances of the play was probably at the entertainment given by James for his brother-in-law, King Christian of Denmark, at Hampton Court in August 1606. In his detailed study of the contemporary backgound of *Macbeth*, H. N. Paul argues that it was written especially for this occasion, and there can be no doubt that Shakespeare intended to please the King with his only Scottish play, and one that included several of James's ancestors among its characters. In contrast to the infertility of the Tudors, the Scottish House of Stuart could boast an unbroken succession of eight monarchs deriving from the marriage of a daughter of Robert the Bruce, descended from Duncan, to Walter Stuart, supposed to be descended from Banquo. This is the royal line celebrated in the show of eight kings in Act IV, scene i of *Macbeth*. If Mary Queen of Scots is omitted from the succession – she had been deposed, and only kings are referred to – the eighth king would be James himself, and the glass he holds showing his descendants compliments the King by predicting the continuation of his line into the distant future. The 'twofold balls and treble sceptres' (IV.i.121) celebrate the union of the English and Scottish thrones – the 'twofold balls' are the two orbs used in the coronation rites in England and in Scotland and there are three sceptres because two were used in the English ceremony.

There was good reason to emphasise the importance of national unity and of an undisputed succession for the well-being of the country. *Macbeth* was written in the aftermath of the discovery in November 1605 of the Gunpowder Plot – the attempt to blow up the King and both houses of Parliament by a group of Catholic gentlemen, made desperate by the fines and restrictions imposed on them for not belonging to the Protestant faith. A plot to murder a king was a highly topical subject, with the country still shaken by reports 'Of dire combustion, and confused events' (II.iii.57), and the play must often have touched on the recent experience of its audience. Lady Macbeth's advice,

> look like the innocent flower,
> But be the serpent under't, (I.v.64-5)

might have recalled the medal struck to commemorate the discovery of the plot, showing a serpent concealed beneath flowers, and Paul suggests that Duncan's comment on the treachery of the Thane of Cawdor,

> There's no art
> To find the mind's construction in the face:
> He was a gentleman on whom I built
> An absolute trust, (I.iv.11-14)

may have been prompted by the complicity in the Plot of Sir Everard Digby, who had been particularly favoured by the King. But it was Father Henry Garnet, Provincial of the English Jesuits, who provided the most striking connection between the play and contemporary events. When he was arrested Garnet denied any knowledge of the Plot and after he had been tricked into admitting his guilt he defended his perjury as 'equivocation' – the telling of deliberately misleading half-truths – and maintained that this was justified in the cause of religion; as the Porter was to put it, he

> committed treason enough for God's sake, yet could not
> equivocate to heaven. (II.iii.10-11)

Garnet did not provide the original hint for Shakespeare's profound treatment of the equivocal nature of evil – it was already implied in the original story of Macbeth by the prophecies that give him false confidence at the end of his reign (see page 61) – but he certainly gave it a very specific relevance at the time of the play's first performances.

The murder, or attempted murder, of a king was regarded with particular horror, as the supreme violation of the principles according to which God had created the universe. Political theory stressed the importance of order in the state, and from the Middle Ages it was assumed that this order should be hierarchical, reflecting the hierarchy of heaven, in which, it was thought, the various ranks of spiritual beings were placed one above the other, ascending to God himself. The natural structure of the state, therefore, was the hierarchy of different social classes with the king at its apex – God's representative on earth. In *Basilicon Doron*, the manual on kingship he wrote for his son, James maintained that not even a tyrant might be lawfully deposed once he had been acknowledged as king.

The same principle of order was to be seen in the natural world, rising from the lowest form of material substance through the vegetable and animal kingdoms to man as its natural ruler, and each subdivision of this great chain of creation was thought to be organised on a similar pattern. Animals, plants, and even inanimate things were ranked according to their status: the sun was the monarch of the physical heavens, the lion of animals, the eagle of birds. Because all these hierarchies mirrored each other there was thought to be a sympathetic relationship, or 'correspondence', between them so that disturbances in one were reflected by disturbances in the others. Thus when the king is murdered it is appropriate that there are sympathetic disturbances in the elements (II.iii.53–60), that the sun is darkened, a falcon killed by a mousing owl, and Duncan's horses turn not only on each other but against their natural superior, man – as the Old Man says,

> 'Tis unnatural,
> Even like the deed that's done. (II.iv.5–18)

We accept such relationships as symbolic, but for the Jacobeans they would also have had a more literal meaning.

Human nature was understood in terms of the same hierarchical principle. Man's physical and mental health depended on the preservation of a harmonious order between his various organs and faculties. Man was a universe in miniature, a 'microcosm' or 'little world' that mirrored and was sympathetically connected with the 'macrocosm' or 'great world'. When Macbeth refers to his 'single state of man' (I.iii.140) – his 'individual state' – he is suggesting this relationship between a political state and the human constitution; his temporary loss of control is seen as a rebellion against him by his physical organs and his imagination. The same conditions were necessary for man's physical and mental health as for the well-being of the country. Reason should rule; when Macbeth's ambition rebels against it his whole constitution becomes disordered, and his kingdom is similarly infected: Scotland needs purging (V.ii.28). Conversely, the legitimate king is 'the medicine of the sickly weal' (V.ii.27). This idea was given literal expression by the belief that the king could cure scrofula – the 'king's evil' – by touching the afflicted person. The efficacy of the king's touch was regarded as evidence of his legitimacy, so although James thought the practice superstitious he continued it in a modified form – as Malcolm describes the ceremony at the court of Edward the Confessor (IV.iii.150–4).

1.3 WITCHCRAFT AND DEMONOLOGY

The antithesis to the divinely ordained order of the universe is represented in *Macbeth* by the Witches. They meet in storms (I.i.1–2) and can raise tempests (I.iii.11–25); they are unnatural themselves – women with beards

(I.iii.45-7) – and they work their spells with fragments torn from organic creatures – the thumb of a pilot (I.iii.28), and the organs of men and animals that make up their charm in IV.i; they symbolise sterility and death by their 'withered' appearance, with 'choppy' fingers and 'skinny lips' (I.iii.40-5), and they reduce their victims to the same condition – as the First Witch plans to revenge the insult given her by the sailor's wife:

> I'll drain him dry as hay: . . .
>
> . . . .
>
> Weary sev'n-nights nine times nine
> Shall he dwindle, peak and pine. (I.iii.18-23)

Their most potent symbol is that of the

> birth-strangled babe
> Ditch-delivered by a drab, (IV.i.30-1)

combining the destruction of new life with the unnatural and inhuman circumstances of the birth by a whore who has perverted the life-giving forces of nature.

In Shakespeare's source the three women who accost Macbeth and Banquo are described as 'the weird sisters' and identified with 'the goddesses of destinie' – 'weird' meaning 'fatal', in the sense of foreseeing or controlling fate. Shakespeare retains the name but transforms them into the familiar witches of the English, or Scottish, countryside, to whose malice any unexplained disease in their neighbours, or their neighbours' livestock (I.iii.2), was often attributed. Witches were not thought to be supernatural beings themselves, but supposedly gained their powers by selling their souls to Satan, and were then instructed and controlled by 'familiar spirits', minor devils which often took the form of birds and animals – like the familiars who summon Shakespeare's witches at the end of I.i, and instruct them when to begin the charm at the beginning of IV.i. It was their familiars who enabled them to ride in the air (IV.i.138), or disappear into it (I.iii.79-82); to raise storms, and to foretell the ι ʾʾre, as do the Apparitions, whom the Witches also call their 'masters' (IV.i.63).

A coven of witches had practised against King James during his voyage from Denmark after his marriage to Anne, King Christian's sister – a circumstance that would have made the play particularly appropriate for the Hampton Court entertainment. One of them confessed that after she had been incited by the Devil to kill the King she had tried unsuccessfully to poison him with the venom collected from a toad (compare IV.i.6-8). She and her coven had then christened a cat, tied to it parts of the body of a dead man (compare IV.i.26,29) and 'sailing in their riddles or sieves' (compare I.iii.8) left it in the sea before the port of Leith. This raised such a storm that one ship was sunk and the King's ship delayed by contrary winds. These proceedings excited James's interest in the subject. In 1597 he wrote a treatise on witchcraft, *Demonologie*, and after his accession to the English throne frequently investigated alleged cases of witchcraft and demonic possession – the supposed entry into a human being by a devil, often at the instigation of a witch.

The existence of witchcraft was recognised by English law – an act of 1604 made the practice of it punishable by death – but it was by no means unquestioned. Reginald Scott had made a forthright attack on the popular beliefs in his *Discoverie of Witchcraft* (1584) and many of those who held to the traditional belief were aware that alleged cases of witchcraft were often fraudulent or the result of neurotic delusions; in 1603 Dr Edward Jordan described in *A Brief Discourse of a Disease called Suffocation, or the Mother* how delusions of demonic possession could be produced by hysteria – or 'the mother', as it was then called. There was considerable interest in the power of the imagination to create such effects; Shakespeare was certainly familiar with Montaigne's essay on 'The Force of the Imagination', published in Florio's translation of the *Essays* in 1603, and possibly with such works as Lavater's *Of Ghosts and Spirits* (English translation, 1572) which may have contributed to the differences of opinion expressed in *Hamlet* about the reality of the Ghost.

There can be little doubt that most of his audience would have believed in witches, and for the purposes of the play, at least, Shakespeare also accepted their reality, but his portrayal of the hallucinatory power of the imagination is perhaps even more compelling. The fusion in *Macbeth* of these two attitudes to demonology, the superstitious and the sceptical, enables it to combine a vivid external presentation of the forces of evil with a profound exploration of their psychological sources and effects in the human mind.

2 SUMMARY AND CRITICAL COMMENTARY

Act I, Scene i

Three Witches arrange to meet Macbeth after the conclusion of a battle that is in progress. When called by their familiar spirits (see page 6) they leave, joining together in a riddling chant.

This scene establishes the atmosphere of mystery and horror and introduces the underlying forces that will control the action of the play. A sense of supernatural evil is conveyed by the thunder and lightning and by the appearance of the Witches – later described by Banquo (I.iii.39–47). Their rhymed tetrameter verse – verse in which each line of seven or eight syllables is divided into four metrical feet – with its emphatic trochaic rhythm, where the accent falls on the first syllable of each foot, sounds like an incantation, and contrasts throughout the play with the blank verse spoken by the other characters. They can foresee the future – they evidently know what the outcome of the battle will be – and their enigmatic speech suggests that they are in touch with knowledge denied to ordinary mortals. We catch only tantalising fragments of information: we do not know the location of the scene or on what heath they will meet Macbeth, what battle is taking place or in what sense it will be 'lost and won' – this might mean merely that the vanquished will lose and the victors win, but the Witches' condensed phrase implies something more than this obvious fact, and the close connection of 'winning' and 'losing' might suggest that the two are indistinguishable, that what seems to be success is really failure, as Macbeth discovers in the course of the play. They already have an interest in him, and he is thus first introduced to the audience in a powerful, if undefined, atmosphere of evil. The paradox of the Witches' final couplet, 'Fair is foul, and foul is fair', sums up the reversal of normal moral values that is the central principle of Satanism – as Satan says in Milton's *Paradise Lost*, 'Evil be thou my good'. This moral confusion is reflected both in the storm in the heavens and in the 'hurlyburly' of the battle on earth.

Act I, Scene ii

The battle referred to by the Witches is revealed to be that against the rebel Macdonwald and the invading army of Sweno, King of Norway, supported by the treacherous Thane of Cawdor. News is brought by a wounded Captain, and by Ross and Angus, of the victories of Macbeth and Banquo. Duncan condemns Cawdor to death and confers his title on Macbeth.

The scene changes from the undefined supernatural setting of I.i to the urgent physical action of the battle. The danger to Scotland, the ferocity of the conflict and the heroism of Macbeth and Banquo are conveyed through the excited interjections of the Captain and the elaborate description: there are extended similes (8–9, 25–8, 35, 37–8) and frequent personifications – of Fortune, Valour and Justice (14–15, 19, 29); Macbeth is 'Valour's minion' (19) and 'Bellona's bridegroom' (54). This formal, 'epic' style gives his achievements an ideal, heroic character, but in no way diminishes the realism of the account. It has a primitive violence: Macbeth 'carved out his passage' and without more ado 'unseamed' Macdonwald 'from the nave to th' chops' (19–22); his sword 'smoked with bloody execution' (18), and both he and Banquo seemed determined 'to bathe in reeking wounds' (39). The scene is full of images of blood – as is the whole play – and the occasional broken lines convey the Captain's own pain and weariness. His wounds and the preliminary 'alarum' introduce vivid fragments of battle into the theatre, and the use of two separate messengers suggests the uncertainty of the outcome – the Captain does not know the result of the second engagement.

Duncan is now too old to lead his forces in person, but clearly commands the respect of his thanes and is prompt to recognise their services; his praise helps to emphasise the nobility of Macbeth. There is dramatic irony (see page 65) in his resolve not to be further deceived by 'that' Thane of Cawdor (64) since he will again be betrayed by the new Thane of Cawdor, and, moreover, it is the transfer of the title to Macbeth that encourages his hopes for the crown (I.iii.127–33). The irony is underlined by the Captain's proverbial observation,

> So from that spring whence comfort seemed to come
> Discomfort swells. Mark, King of Scotland, mark. (27–8)

This would not be apparent until the next scene, but there is a faintly ominous echo of the Witches' 'When the battle's lost and won' in Duncan's last line. Macbeth's winning of this title will lead to 'loss' not only for Duncan but for himself.

Act I, Scene iii

While waiting to meet Macbeth the Witches plot their revenge on a sailor's wife, who has insulted one of them. Macbeth enters with Banquo and they salute him as Thane of Glamis (his former title), Thane of Cawdor (his new title, not yet publicly announced), and as the future king. When Banquo challenges them to foretell his future they reply paradoxically that he will be lesser than Macbeth, but greater, less happy, but happier, and although not a king himself will be the father of kings. Macbeth wishes to hear more, but the Witches vanish. Ross and Angus enter with the news that Macbeth has been created Thane of Cawdor and this sudden fulfilment of the Witches' prediction raises his hopes that their prophecy that he will be king will also be fulfilled; the idea of murdering Duncan immerses him in agitated thought. He is recalled to present affairs by Banquo and they agree to discuss further what has happened.

The supernatural atmosphere of I.i is recreated by the Witches' account of their malignant activities and by their charm (32-7) with its nine-fold ritual - the magical power of the number nine has already appeared in the fate they plan for the sailor (22). Their power is limited; they cannot destroy the sailor's bark, although they can persecute him in ways that anticipate the effect they will have on Macbeth, who will also be deprived of sleep and drained 'dry as hay' (18-25). Equally, they cannot corrupt the virtuous, they can only work on the evil they find already in their victims' minds. Thus it is significant that they only prophesy that Macbeth will be king, without suggesting how this will be accomplished; it is Macbeth who thinks of murder. This, and the guilty start that Banquo notices (51), suggest that the thought was already in the back of his mind. His first words in the play - probably a casual comment on the weather - echo the Witches' 'Fair is foul, and foul is fair' (I.i.11) as if he were unconsciously in tune with them; and almost immediately his own moral confusion is betrayed by the alarm with which he reacts to 'Things that do sound so fair' (51-2) and by his uncertainty as to whether this approach by the Witches is good or evil (130-1).

The speeches of Ross and Angus remind us of the impression of Macbeth built up in the previous scene as the self-sufficient warrior, single-minded in his loyalty, but almost as soon as he appears in person we see a totally different Macbeth, at first startled and uneasy, and then, when one prophecy of the Witches is unexpectedly fulfilled, shaken by the conflict between the grandeur of his ambition - 'the swelling act Of the imperial theme' (128-9) - and the horrifying thought of Duncan's murder. According to Ross, he was 'Nothing afeard' of the 'Strange images of death' that he produced externally on the battlefield (96-7), but now he is overwhelmed by the 'horrid image' of Duncan's murder in his own mind (135). It seems to rise involuntarily in his imagination, attacking his physical being, 'unfixing' his hair and making his 'seated heart' knock at his ribs. Neither his body nor his mind is fully under his control; already there is a powerful sense of psychological disintegration under the stress of his moral conflict. The unity of his personality, his 'single state of man', is 'shaken' by the thought of murder. Mere 'imaginings' have more reality for him than the actually existing present, so that 'function' - his power of action -

> Is smothered in surmise, and nothing is
> But what is not. (137–42)

This paradoxical statement is central to the play. Its simple meaning is that nothing is real for Macbeth except the prospect of future kingship, which 'is not' in the sense that it exists only in his fantasy. But its implications resonate through the play. Macbeth's confusion of what 'is not' for what 'is' is clearly related to his mistaking false appearances for reality - preferring the illusions of grandeur offered by the Witches to the real honour he gains by serving Duncan, and launching himself on a course of self-destruction because he thinks it is the way to more complete self-fulfilment (see pages 26 and 30).

Of course, neither the audience nor Macbeth is explicitly aware of these implications at the time. They are only hinted at, and the compressed, indirect expression of the second half of this speech reflects his unwillingness to look squarely at the action that has suggested itself to him. To escape this thought that dominates his imagination he turns with relief to the simple reflection,

> If chance will have me king, why, chance may crown me,
> Without my stir, (143–4)

which is the obvious conclusion to draw from the Witches' prophecy, yet he never returns to it again.

Macbeth's introverted musing contrasts with the open, formal speech of Ross and Angus, and the contrast is highlighted by their easy conversation with Banquo. Macbeth is at first unable even to acknowledge their praises adequately, throwing them a curt word of thanks and emphasising its inadequacy by repeating it a few lines later (117, 129). He is not a good dissembler, and the stirrings of guilt are already beginning to separate him from ordinary human society. Banquo tries genially to excuse his behaviour by picking up Macbeth's accusation that they were dressing him in 'borrowed robes' (109) and suggesting that his new honours

> Like our strange garments, cleave not to their mould
> But with the aid of use (145-6)

- an image that becomes highly significant when Macbeth is, metaphorically, dressed instead in stolen garments (V.ii.20-2).

The contrast between the reactions of Macbeth and Banquo to the Witches is also striking. Banquo is certainly more open in his response. It is he who describes their appearance, with even a touch of mockery in his reference to their beards (39-47), and questions whether they are only an illusion (53-47, 83-5). The imagery he uses –

> If you can look into the seeds of time,
> And say which grain will grow, and which will not (58-9)

– gives a serious tone to his demand to be told his fate and pointedly anticipates their prophecy about his 'seed' (compare III.i.69); but compared with Macbeth's desire for more information (75-8) and his brooding 'Would they had stayed!' (82) his comments after the Witches' disappearance seem light-hearted, especially the humorous, 'To the selfsame tune and words' (88). Banquo can be played in various ways. When he notices Macbeth's guilty start (51-2) is he merely surprised, or suspicious about its cause? Does his reaction to the news that Macbeth is Thane of Cawdor – 'What, can the devil speak true?' – express sceptical amusement, or some foreboding of evil? It may be relevant that he does not speak this openly. How much importance does he attach to Macbeth's question, 'Do you not hope your children shall be kings. . .?' (118) – it obviously weighs with Macbeth as he had used identical words a little earlier (86). It may be significant that Banquo avoids answering directly, and his retort,

> That, trusted home,
> Might yet enkindle you unto the crown, (120-1)

might be either an innocent observation or an indication that he suspects Macbeth's intentions. He is well aware of the danger of taking words that 'sound so fair' (52) at their face value; it is he who sums up with characteristic clearsightedness the deceitfulness of evil temptation:

> And oftentimes, to win us to our harm,
> The instruments of darkness tell us truths,
> Win us with honest trifles, to betray's
> In deepest consequence. (123-6)

Act I, Scene iv

Malcolm describes the execution of the Thane of Cawdor to Duncan, who comments on the impossibility of knowing a man's character from his outward appearance, as he had placed complete trust in him. When Macbeth enters he praises him effusively and promises to reward both him and Banquo; he creates Malcolm Prince of Cumberland, and so heir to the throne, and announces his intention of visiting Macbeth at Inverness. As Macbeth leaves to inform his wife of the royal visit he reflects that

Malcolm's elevation bars his own way to the throne and braces himself to overcome this obstacle.

This scene in Duncan's court is in appropriately formal style: the speeches are elaborate and courtly – Macbeth's perhaps too self-consciously so with their elaborate stress on loyalty, duty and the joy of serving the King. Again we see 'the gracious Duncan' – as Macbeth is later to call him (III.i.65) – eager to acknowledge his debt to Macbeth, warmly embracing Banquo, and moved to tears by the loyalty of his thanes. This apparent harmony is reinforced by the natural images in which the relation of monarch to subject is described: for Macbeth it is that of father to children (24-5), and both Duncan and Banquo speak of the King's favour in terms of biological growth and harvest (28-9, 32-3).

At the same time, the King might seem here to be revealing some of the weakness of the historical Duncan (see page 62). There is obvious dramatic irony when his bland reflections on the ease with which one can be deceived by appearances are immediately followed by the entry of the new Thane of Cawdor, in whom Duncan is evidently prepared to place an equally 'absolute trust' (14); he has learnt nothing from his misjudgement of the former Thane. There is further irony when, in the general distribution of honours to his loyal thanes, he names Malcolm as his successor and so prompts one of them to plot his murder, and then provides the ideal opportunity by visiting his castle.

After his anguished contemplation of murder in the previous scene, Macbeth's final aside (48-53) reveals a new determination, reflected in the grim movement of the lines – the rhymed verse perhaps recalling the incantations of the Witches. The simple, direct language – the speech is almost entirely monosyllabic – contrasts with the elaborate style of the rest of the scene. 'Stars, hide your fires' recalls the 'stars' to which Duncan compared the 'signs of nobleness' that would 'shine On all deservers' (41-2); Macbeth is prepared to relinquish the honours he has deservedly gained for the supreme honour of kingship that he can now obtain only by furtive concealment. Similarly, the earlier imagery of biological growth is replaced by an unnatural dislocation of his bodily functions, 'The eye wink at the hand'. It is as if Macbeth wishes his hand to act independently of himself, to dissociate himself from the blow it must strike. The tension of steeling himself to murder is increasing the disintegration of his personality; if he could he would conceal his intention even from himself.

The irony of the scene as a whole is emphasised by framing this murderous aside between Duncan's farewell, 'My worthy Cawdor' (47), and his final words to Banquo which show that while Macbeth is preparing himself for murder his intended victim is relishing the praises of the murderer. Duncan does not envisage the way in which Macbeth will prove 'worthy' as the successor to the treacherous Cawdor.

Act I, Scene v

At Inverness Lady Macbeth is reading Macbeth's letter informing her of the Witches' prophecies. She determines that he will be king, and fearing that his moral scruples will prevent him from achieving his ambition in the most direct way she is anxious to inspire him with her own ruthlessness. A messenger brings the news of Duncan's visit and she summons the forces of darkness to destroy in her any trace of feminine sympathy. When Macbeth enters she greets him rapturously and insists that Duncan shall never leave the castle alive. She advises him to conceal his intentions with an appearance of hospitality, assures him that she will organise the murder, and dismisses his suggestion that they discuss the matter further.

Lady Macbeth presents a masterly account of her husband's character; her first soliloquy (14–29) is in fact an extended commentary on his aside at the end of the previous scene, analysing his wish to enjoy the fruits of murder without actually committing it himself:

> that which rather thou dost fear to do
> Than wishest should be undone (23–4)

is almost an exact repetition of his

> yet let that be
> Which the eye fears, when it is done, to see. (I.iv.52–3)

Her own determination is expressed with magnificent assurance, 'and shalt be What thou art promised' (14–15); she feels 'The future in the instant' (56–7), as did Macbeth (I.iii.137–42), but with none of the horror or psychological disturbance that he had experienced. She dismisses any religious considerations with the contemptuous jingle, 'What thou wouldst highly, That wouldst though holily', and is undeterred by the unnaturalness of the evil she contemplates, describing it cynically as an 'illness', a perversion of human nature. This is anticipated by her complaint that her husband is 'too full o' th' milk of human kindness', for 'human kindness' means not only 'human compassion', but also 'human nature' – the meaning of 'kind' that survives today in 'mankind'; we still use 'humanity' in the double sense of 'human beings' and 'compassion' – the feeling appropriate to a human being – and speak of cruelty as 'inhuman'. Thus in seeking to eradicate Macbeth's sense of pity she is seeking to destroy his human nature. The whole soliloquy, in its approval of evil ambition and contempt for moral principles, endorses the inverted values of the Witches (I.i.11). It is the more horrifying for the cool detachment with which Lady Macbeth assesses her husband's potential as a murderer beneath her intense determination that he shall realise that potential.

The entry of the messenger is highly dramatic, and even Lady Macbeth is momentarily thrown off balance by the news that the ideal opportunity for the murder will be that very night (30). Is she perhaps startled by the way in which his message chimes in with her guilty intentions, as Macbeth started when the Witches' prophecy seemed to express his secret thoughts? She recovers immediately, with the grim comment on the croaking of the raven, but she is aware of her own capacity for pity (39–49), and like Macbeth she has to steel herself for the murder – crush her own humanity, be unsexed, sterilised of feminine feelings, her milk (continuing the imagery she had used of her husband) converted into gall. The 'spirits That tend on mortal thoughts' that she summons are the familiar spirits that attended witches and controlled men and women in a state of demonic possession (see page 7); as she had echoed the perverted doctrine of the Witches in her first soliloquy, so she is now demanding the characteristics of a witch, to be possessed by evil. Both Macbeth and Lady Macbeth become dehumanised by their crimes, but while the murderous thoughts that shook his 'state of man' (I.iii.140) were encouraged by his unintentional meeting with the Witches she deliberately calls the 'murd'ring ministers' to her: she sees what she must become in order to murder, and wills it to happen. Similarly, while both of them summon darkness to conceal their intentions (49–53; I.iv.50–3) he wants it to hide the murder from his own eyes, she to hide it, metaphorically, from the knife she uses – she, herself, is more steely than the knife.

When Macbeth enters she echoes the formal threefold greeting the Witches had given him (53–4). She ignores his recent victories and begins to pour her spirits in his ear (25) by preventing him from thinking of anything but the promise of the throne. Their brief conversation is highly charged. Are his first two speeches mere statements of fact, or is the first heavy with sinister implications, and the 'he' of the second stressed to imply that their purposes will be very different? One's interpretation will depend on how far he seems to have lost the resolution he showed at the end of I.iv, for the expression on his face, noticed by his wife (61–2), shows that he has lost some of it, and so does his temporising reply, 'We will speak further' (70). He wishes to avoid an immediate decision, while she is all for action. There is no doubt about the menacing irony of her curt question, 'And when goes hence?' (58), or of the grim puns on 'provided for' – they must prepare both to entertain Duncan and to murder him – and 'despatch' – both the 'business' and Duncan must be despatched (66–7). She may even be thinking of killing him herself – she referred to 'my' keen knife (51) – but her final words, 'Leave all the rest to me', are probably only to reassure Macbeth that she will make all the necessary arrangements. She is already instructing him on the need for concealment (62–5); they are entering a world of deception, and of self-deception: even now she tactfully avoids the word 'murder', speaking instead of 'This night's great business' (67), and one hears her exultation in the resonant couplet,

> Which shall to all our nights and days to come
> Give solely sovereign sway and masterdom. (68-9)

Act I, Scene vi

Duncan with his attendant lords arrives at Macbeth's castle and is welcomed by Lady Macbeth.

The scene moves outside the castle, from discordant plotting to the harmony of oboes, from the darkness invoked by the Macbeths to the welcoming light of torches, and from the tenseness of their dialogue to the relaxed conversation of Duncan and Banquo as they describe its agreeable setting. Both emphasise the limpid quality of the 'delicate' air (10) – it 'Smells wooingly' (6) and

> Nimbly and sweetly recommends itself
> Unto our gentle senses (2-3)

– in marked contrast to the 'thick night' invoked by Lady Macbeth (I.v.49), and the 'fog and filthy air' of the witches (I.i.12). The castle seems to be following her advice and looking like the 'innocent flower' (I.v.64); instead of the ominous raven (I.v.37-9) there are only the martlets (martins). Banquo's description of them is particularly engaging. He stresses their fertility – their nests are 'procreant cradles' and 'Where they most breed and haunt. . . The air is delicate' (8-10) – recalling the imagery of growth and harvest he had used with Duncan to describe the reward of loyal service in a well-ordered kingdom (I.iv.28-33), in contrast to Lady Macbeth's sterile imagery of disease and perversion as she plotted to overthrow the natural order in the state. The martlets are 'temple-haunting' (4) and the reference to the air as 'heaven's breath' (5) suffuses the scene with a sense of divine order, the condition for healthy growth both in the natural world and in the state. The movement of the speech is fluent and leisurely; it is a brief moment of repose in the tense action of the play.

The martlets, however, have a further significance. 'Martin' was a slang term for a dupe, and in *The Merchant of Venice* the martlet that builds its nest in a dangerously exposed position on the outside of a wall is compared to a man who judges by outward appearances. They are an apt symbol for Duncan and Banquo at this moment, unsuspicious of the danger within the castle, and one is reminded of Duncan's inability 'To find the mind's construction in the face' (I.iv.12).

With the entry of Lady Macbeth the elaborate exchange of courtesies stresses the mutual affection between monarch and subject. Duncan apologises humorously for the trouble his visit is causing, pointing out that it results from his love for his hosts, just as he himself is sometimes overburdened by the attentions of his loving subjects (11-14). The irony of his misinterpretation of the reason for Macbeth's haste is pointed by the simile he uses, 'sharp as his spur' (23). Lady Macbeth is even more extravagant than her husband had been (I.iv.22–27) in protesting that any services they can do the King are inadequate repayment of the debt they owe him, and there is repeated reference to her role as hostess (10, 24–5, 31). Significantly, Macbeth absents himself from this formal welcome.

Act I, Scene vii

Macbeth has withdrawn from the banquet that he is giving for Duncan (29) and in an anguished soliloquy decides not to proceed with the murder, but Lady Macbeth persuades him to change his mind.

In contrast to the sociable activity of the banquet, presented on stage by the oboes and torches, and the coming and going of the sewer and the servants, Macbeth is again isolated in guilty reflections, as he had been from the cheerful conversation of his colleagues in I.iii. His soliloquy (1–28) reveals the nature of his mental conflict with remarkable subtlety. He tells himself that he is concerned only with the practical question of whether or not he can get away with the murder, and he explicitly dismisses its moral aspects: if it were over and done with once it was committed, if the act of killing Duncan, by giving him supreme power, would prevent any repercussions on himself in this life, then he would ignore the possibility of divine retribution after death, in 'the life to come' (1–7). But the inadequacy of this tough-minded attitude is exposed by the very imagery with which he expresses it. His description of this world, temporal life, as a 'bank and shoal of time' (6) emphasises its impermanence; it is no more stable or reliable than a sandbank in the sea of eternity – 'the life to come' (7) – that will be submerged or washed away by that sea. The image implies what Macbeth really knows to be true, that it is eternal spiritual values that matter, not transitory earthly success, and however hard he tries to repress this deeper insight it expresses itself involuntarily through the images springing from his imagination. The conflict between the implications of this image and his explicit reasoning is a vivid realisation of the division within himself that results from his attempt to assume a false role.

Through the rest of the soliloquy this spiritual insight becomes more explicit and the imagery expressing it more insistent. Macbeth is fully aware of his threefold obligation to Duncan, as subject, kinsman and host (13–16), and of Duncan's virtues – he has been 'So clear in his great office' (18), a clarity that contrasts both with Macbeth's secret plotting and with the confusion of his mind and attempts to cloud his own moral awareness. Again, he pretends to be considering the immorality of the murder only as a reason for supposing that it will be avenged: by killing Duncan he will merely be showing others how to kill him (7–12), there will be such universal distress at the treacherous murder of so virtuous a king (12–25). But the imagery that dominates his mind shows that he himself is equally horrified. Duncan's virtues will 'plead like angels trumpet-tongued'; pity, the softest of emotions, compared to a 'naked new-born babe', is given cosmic force when it is 'Striding the blast'; and 'heaven's cherubim', often represented as winged infants, become swift agents of divine vengeance, 'horsed Upon the sightless couriers of the air' (18–23). The fusion of helpless innocence with violent power evokes a terrifying apocalyptic vision shot through with suggestions of the Last Judgement and that spiritual retribution that Macbeth affected to despise at the beginning of the soliloquy: Duncan's murder is a 'deep damnation' (20), the 'trumpet-tongued' angels recall the angelic trumpeters who will summon mankind for final judgement, and the 'blast' (22) of the tempest is an extension of their accusing trumpet blasts. It is an overwhelming expression of the power of those humane feelings that Lady Macbeth had dismissed as 'th' milk of human kindness' (I.v.16), a phrase recalled by the image of the new-born babe. Macbeth's imagination has dramatised for him the spiritual horror that he is contemplating; by line 25, in fact, his practical argument has been left behind and there remain only the tears of pity, which he shares. His conclusion is in the practical vein in which he began – his ambition will make him over-reach himself and cause his downfall (25–8) – but *only* Vaulting ambition' indicates that he recognises the insignificance of wordly ambition compared to the spiritual forces unleashed in his imagination.

This soliloquy penetrates deeply into Macbeth's personality, the imagery revealing subconscious depths beneath his surface reasoning. However, he does not venture to raise any of this with his wife; when she enters he justifies his decision not to murder Duncan on the practical grounds that they should make the most of the honours he has recently gained (32–5). The dialogue that follows is as revealing by what they do not say as by what they do.

Lady Macbeth attacks at once; she uses various means to make him change his mind, including a passing appeal – or challenge – to his love (38–9), but she focuses on his most sensitive point, his courage – the quality that had won him the 'Golden opinions' (33) that he has just advanced as a reason for not proceeding with the murder. She picks up his metaphor of clothing (34–5) and flings it back derisively, 'Was the hope drunk Wherein you dressed yourself?' and then answers his argument directly by accusing him of wanting to enjoy a reputation for courage while knowing that he is really a coward (41–3). She exploits the insight into his character which she showed in her first soliloquy (I.v.14–24), the conclusions of which are condensed in her scornful question,

> Art thou afeard
> To be the same in thine own act and valour
> As thou art in desire? (39–41; compare I.v.23–4)

She attributes his hesitation, however, only to cowardice, without mentioning the moral scruples that she knows him to have – and that Macbeth himself seems reluctant to raise with her, perhaps fearing her scorn. Their relationship has not developed at this deeper level. He is sufficiently stung by her accusation to state the central moral issue,

> I dare do all that may become a man;
> Who dares do more is none. (46–7)

By seeking to rise above humanity, to escape the obligations of ordinary human beings, one merely destroys one's human nature (see page 59) – but his protest seems half-hearted and she brushes it aside with her own concept of manhood as irresponsible self-assertion and follows this with a demonstration of her own 'masculine' strength in terrible lines (54–9) that recall her demand to be 'unsexed', to have her milk turned to gall (I.v.39–49).

At the same time she places her husband in a false position by asserting that it was he who first suggested the murder and was determined to contrive an opportunity for it (47–52). One cannot know how true this is. It must refer to a period before the beginning of the play since by the time they meet on stage 'time' and 'place' have already 'made themselves' (51, 53) – Duncan is visiting them and providing the perfect time and place. Macbeth has certainly considered the murder before he meets the Witches (see page 11) and Lady Macbeth may be justified in claiming that he previously displayed a resolution that has evaporated now that he is faced with the opportunity to act (53–4), but equally she might be exaggerating his earlier commitment to the murder in order to goad him into action.

Macbeth can only respond, almost sheepishly, 'If we should fail?' (59), and his wife promptly changes tactics and outlines a plan of action to show how easy it will be, reassuring him as she had at the end of I.v by taking over the management of the murder (61–72); in effect she is presenting him with a course of action that it is easier for him to follow than it would be to oppose her will. She has poured her spirits in his ear (I.v.25) to such effect that he now speaks with her voice, endorsing her concept of manhood – 'Bring forth men-children only!' (72); enlarging with apparent enthusiasm on her plan – it is he who suggests marking Duncan's attendants with blood and using their daggers (74–7); and repeating in his final cynical couplet the advice that she had previously given him (I.v.62–5, 70–1). But the tension he feels is evident in his need to

> bend up
> Each corporal agent to this terrible feat; (79–80)

even Lady Macbeth feels it when she urges him, 'But screw your courage to the sticking-place' (60), as the cord of a crossbow is stretched taut before it despatches the shaft, or the string of a musical instrument is screwed up to the right pitch until it is in danger of snapping.

Act II, Scene i

Banquo is walking restlessly with Fleance in the night. Meeting Macbeth, he tells him of Duncan's pleasure at his reception and hands him a diamond, the King's gift for Lady Macbeth. Macbeth cautiously tests how much support he is likely to get from Banquo and Banquo replies guardedly. As Macbeth waits for the bell by which his wife will signal that the coast is clear for the murder he sees an imaginary dagger pointing towards Duncan's chamber and becoming stained with blood. The bell sounds and he goes to commit the murder.

The Witches have had a malign effect on Banquo as well as on Macbeth. He is afraid to sleep because of the dreams they have stimulated and his nerves are on edge; he calls for his sword when someone approaches even though he is in a supposedly friendly castle (7-9). He may already be un- easy about Macbeth's intentions, although there was no indication of this when he arrived at the castle, and his own ambitions have probably been aroused by the Witches' prediction for him. It is striking, however, that while Macbeth consciously embraces evil and it is his subconscious mind that provides the moral prompting, with Banquo the situation is reversed: consciously he resists any evil impulses, calling on heavenly powers for help (7-9); it is only when his conscious control is relaxed in sleep that 'cursed thoughts' trouble his dreams. His frankness in admitting that he has dreamt of the Witches contrasts with Macbeth's pretence that he has dis- missed them from his thoughts (20-1), and his response to Macbeth's attempt to enlist his support has a firm moral assurance (26-9). It is related to the interchange between Macbeth and Lady Macbeth on the nature of manhood (I.vii.46-51): by trying to rise above what becomes a man one loses one's manhood, by grasping at too much honour one will behave dishonourably. Again one sees Banquo's direct, ingenuous nature. 'Franchised' means free of guilt and so free and open in his behaviour, and his concern that his allegiance should be 'clear' - unsullied - recalls how Duncan had been 'So clear in his great office' (I.vii.18) and that atmospheric clarity that appealed to both Duncan and Banquo on their arrival at Macbeth's castle (I.vi.1-10).

When Banquo has gone Macbeth's taut nerves, screwed 'to the sticking- place' (I.vii.60), create the hallucination of a dagger. His hands and his eyes are at odds (34-7), but the image his imagination conjures up is no longer one of moral condemnation but of murder, and he has the self- control to dismiss it as an illusion (47-9). Through the rest of the speech there is a grim acceptance of the horror of the deed as he dwells on the evil associations of the night that shrouds it; even the stars are hidden

(4-5), as he had demanded (I.iv.50-1). The apparent death of nature, as the natural world sleeps in the half of the globe covered by night (49-50), suits the unnaturalness of the deed; night releases both the witches for the celebration of their queen and the wicked dreams they prompt, as they have in Banquo's sleep. The personification of 'withered Murder' (52) suggests a character in a morality play (see p. 63), and Macbeth identifies himself with it: as he describes its movement he is moving similarly – '*thus* with his stealthy pace' (54). He is losing his personal identity and becoming simply a murderer. 'Withered' reinforces the idea of evil as essentially sterile, already seen in Lady Macbeth's wish to be unsexed (I.v.40), in the 'withered' appearance of the Witches and in their threat to drain the sailor 'dry as hay' (I.iii.40, 18), reducing him to a mere husk. A similar lack of substance is suggested by the comparison of his stealthy movement to that of a ghost (56), a wraith drawn back to earth by some mastering purpose. His whole personality subdued to one evil intention – 'Each corporal agent' bent up 'to this terrible feat' (I.vii.79-80) – Macbeth moves with the inflexible mindlessness of an automaton, and the movement is felt in the steady, hypnotic progression of the verse.

While this soliloquy builds up the setting for the murder and reveals Macbeth's state of mind, it is also dramatising the conflict between appearance and reality that is at the centre of the moral theme of the play. Macbeth knows that the dagger directing him to the murder (42) is an illusion, but he follows it, as he pursues the illusory rewards offered by the forces of evil. He has entered a world of deceptive dreams and he moves through it like a sleep-walker controlled by evil. Contrasting with this unreality is the 'sure and firm-set earth'; he fears that the very stones will betray him and disrupt the atmosphere of supernatural horror which he has braced himself to accept (56-60).

The bell rings, and Macbeth goes to kill Duncan, still with the diamond that the King has given Lady Macbeth. The two cynical couplets (60-1, 63-4) mark the final hardening of his heart; but he still averts his eyes from the murder as his thoughts move directly from 'I go' to the relief of 'it is done' (62), leaving unspoken the deed performed by his hands (compare I.iv.52).

Act II, Scene ii

Lady Macbeth waits nervously for Macbeth's return from Duncan's chamber. He enters with his hands stained with blood and shattered by the deed he has committed, obsessed by his inability to respond with 'Amen' when he heard two of Duncan's train in prayer and by an imaginary voice that he thought he heard proclaim that he had murdered sleep and so would sleep no more. Lady Macbeth scornfully dismisses these fears, tells him to wash and, noticing that he still has the daggers, orders him to return them and smear the faces of Duncan's attendants with blood. When he refuses she takes them herself. As she leaves a knocking is heard on an outer gate of the castle and continues intermittently as Macbeth contemplates his blood-stained hands with horror. Lady Macbeth returns with her hands also stained with blood and eventually persuades him to prepare to meet their guests as if they have been aroused from sleep.

The murder is performed off-stage, but the tension as Lady Macbeth waits anxiously is all the greater, and is increased by the shriek of the owl and the eerie sound of crickets (3, 15), and by Macbeth's disturbing cry off-stage (8). She appears more human here: she is glad to have her courage fortified by alcohol (1), and her reason for not killing Duncan herself shows a capacity for ordinary human feeling – it is perhaps surprising that she should have noticed the resemblance (12–13). Her nervousness is increased by her enforced inactivity. She is startled by the owl but quickly recovers as she compares it grimly to 'the fatal bellman' – the watchman who, in the early sixteenth century, would toll his bell outside the prison in which a criminal was awaiting execution. She rehearses her preparations for the murder (5–8) to reassure herself that nothing could go wrong, but when Macbeth's cry makes her fear that the plot has failed her attempt to convince herself that he could not miss the daggers (12) has a note of desperation. Her exclamation 'My husband!' is ambiguous; does it express triumph, relief, or concern at his distraught appearance?

Macbeth left to kill Duncan with the steady fixation of a sleep-walker; he returns even more wrapt in his own thoughts and moved by a still more terrible compulsion. He and his wife hardly make contact with each other: he does not answer her question (16) and seems to ignore her answer to his (19–20). The single words and short phrases, the sudden shifts of direction, communicate only his tense abstraction. He is still in the nightmare world of the murder, which is given a peculiarly macabre quality by the combination of 'one did laugh in's sleep, and one cried "Murder!"' (22); and his imagination has reasserted its moral power. He dwells on his inability to say 'Amen', as a sign that he is finally excluded from divine grace, with almost childish questioning (31–3). The comparison that he previously made between sleep and death (II.i.49–50) and that Lady Macbeth twice repeats in this scene (7–8, 53–4) is now reversed. By killing Duncan in his sleep Macbeth has murdered sleep, and sleep is now identified with the life-giving forces – 'great nature' (39) – that both he and his wife have rejected: it refreshes, it smooths out the tangles of the day, it is a source of nourishment, the second course in the banquet of life (37–40). Previously he had wished that his hands could carry out the murder of their own accord without his seeing it (I.iv.52); now he regards his blood-stained hands as if, indeed, they were not his own – 'What hands are here?' – but so far from being hidden from him, they pluck out his eyes (59), as the physical action he has forced himself to take is tearing at his moral insight. The conflict between his physical organs, his eyes and hands, reflects the progress of his psychological disintegration; and at the end of the scene the division produced within him by the murder is complete and is stated explicitly, 'To know my deed, 'twere best not know myself' (73).

The interchange with Lady Macbeth opens with nervous, staccato phrases, but as Macbeth's imagination develops the moral significance of the experiences he has suffered, agitation is replaced by compulsive horror; the verse progressively broadens as he enlarges on the blessings of sleep (35–40) and hears his denunciation resounding through the castle (41-3), and the movement culminates in the tremendous image that relates his blood-stained hands to the indelible stain on his character:

> Will all great Neptune's ocean wash this blood
> Clean from my hand? No, this my hand will rather
> The multitudinous seas incarnadine,
> Making the green one red. (60-3)

The conviction felt in the magnificent polysyllabic movement of 'multi-tudinous seas incarnadine' is clinched by the simplicity with which the idea is repeated in the line that follows.

Lady Macbeth attempts to dismiss Macbeth's fears with her nonchalant 'I heard the owl scream, and the crickets cry' (15), the contemptuous 'A foolish thought, to say a sorry sight' (21), and the casually matter-of-fact, 'There are two lodged together' (25). Her rebukes become more explicit,

> These deeds must not be thought
> After these ways; so, it will make us mad (33-4)

– an ironic anticipation of her own fate – but she has temporarily lost control of her husband and can only interject a feeble 'What do you mean?' (40) as he expatiates on sleep. Even when she rounds on him, accusing him of cowardice, and suddenly notices that he still holds the daggers (44-9), she cannot compel him to return them. Instead she tries to shame him with another demonstration of her 'manhood', returning the daggers her-self, with a cynical pun on 'gild' and 'guilt' (56-7), and on her return showing her hands to be equally stained with blood; his imaginative con-viction of the inadequacy of the 'multitudinous seas' to cleanse his guilt is exactly balanced by the practical confidence of her 'A little water clears us of this deed' (67). She again tries to reassure him as at the end of I.vii – 'How easy is it then!' (68) – and she finally manages to goad him into action, but Macbeth seems hardly to notice her as he leaves immersed in bitter regret: 'Wake Duncan with thy knocking! I would thou couldst.'

The knocking gives additional urgency to the conclusion of the scene, reinforcing both Macbeth's sense of guilt and Lady Macbeth's desperate efforts to persuade him to take elementary precautions against discovery. From the beginning of I.v, with a brief intermission in I.vi, we have been confined within the Macbeths' castle, and within their minds, entering deeply into Macbeth's consciousness as we share his moral conflict and experience the hallucinatory images forced up from the less conscious levels of his mind. The knocking disrupts this claustrophobic atmosphere; it is the external world breaking into this realm of evil unreality and illusory values, as daylight begins to disperse the darkness shrouding the castle with its moral clarity and the threat of retribution.

Act II, Scene iii
The knocking continues more loudly as the scene moves to an outer court-yard and sets off a train of wry satire in the mind of the Porter. He eventually admits Macduff and Lennox, who are joined by Macbeth. Macduff leaves to attend on Duncan, while Lennox talks to Macbeth of the tempestuous night, and returns horrified by the murder of the King. Macbeth and Lennox go to see it for themselves while Macduff rouses the castle. On their return, Lennox reports that the culprits appear to have been Duncan's attendants, whom Macbeth has now killed, an action he excuses by his loyal fury at the sight of the murdered king. Lady Macbeth faints, and under cover of this distraction Malcolm and Donalbain discuss the threat to their own safety. Banquo proposes that they meet to inquire into the murder and declares that he will resist the murderer's treacherous intentions. Malcolm and Donalbain decide to fly secretly, Malcolm to England and Donalbain to Ireland.

There is some relaxation of tension with the entrance of the Porter – still suffering from his carousing (23–4), shuffling on his clothes and indignant at being aroused – but so far from providing mere 'comic relief' he presents a grotesque commentary on the tragic action; a Jacobean audience would readily have appreciated the serious intention of this black comedy (see page 63). His fantasy of hell-gate has a grim appropriateness to his actual office, as porter to a castle whose master and mistress have just taken the decisive step towards their own damnation – following what they supposed to be 'the primrose way' that actually leads to 'th' everlasting bonfire' (18–19). The three individuals he fancies he is admitting to hell have all over-reached themselves, like Macbeth: the farmer hoping for an excessive profit by hoarding grain, until the expectation of a plentiful harvest drove down its price and ruined him; the tailor by trying to steal cloth that had been ordered for French hose, which were so close fitting that any reduction in the amount used would be noticed; the equivocator by intending to deceive not only human but also divine justice and 'equivocate to heaven' (11). His comments combine old jokes against farmers and tailors with topical allusions that help to generalise the action of the play by relating it to the contemporary interests of Shakespeare's audience. The equivocator combines the most pointed of these allusions (see page 4) with one of the play's major themes. Equivocation is fundamental to its presentation of evil. Banquo has already described how the 'instruments of darkness' equivocate (I.iii.124–6), and this is one way in which the Witches' inverted moral doctrine (I.i.11) may be understood: they delude with 'Things that do sound so fair' (I.iii.52) but in effect prove to be 'foul' – as they deceive Macbeth with promises of regal grandeur that lead only to the empty form, not the substance, of kingship, and finally destroy him by their misleading prophecies (V.v.42–6, viii.19–22).

The Porter's banter with Macduff (21–40) is equally pointed. His bawdy account of the effect of drink on lechery – 'it provokes the desire, but it takes away the performance' (28–9) – is a burlesque repetition of Lady Macbeth's description of her husband, desiring the crown but unable to perform the actions necessary to achieve it (I.v.14–24), and recalls her comment on his change of mind, 'Was the hope drunk Wherein you dressed yourself?' (I.vii.35–6). Macbeth and Lady Macbeth are deceived by dreams of greatness so that their ambition over-reaches itself and 'falls on the other' (I.vii.27–8), just as drink deceives the Porter's drunkard when it 'equivocates him in a sleep' before 'giving him the lie' (34–5).

The Porter's tardiness gives Macbeth time to regain an appearance of composure. The brevity of his replies shows he is ill at ease, but his response to Lennox's description of the portents that accompanied the murder has a nonchalence worthy of his wife: ''Twas a rough night' (60). With the return of Macduff the external world, heralded by the knocking on the gate, finally bursts in. The knocking is replaced by the clanging of the alarum bell and the stage rapidly fills with distracted characters. Macbeth's vision of the horrified reaction that the murder would excite (I.vii.16–25) is being realised, and is voiced by Macduff. 'The Lord's anointed temple' (67) is Duncan's body, anointed with oil at his coronation, the temple in which divine authority resides on earth. His murder is a sacrilege, and its association with the Last Judgement suggested by the accusing images conjured up by Macbeth's imagination (see page 19) is now stated explicitly. It is 'The great doom's image' – a representation of Judgement Day both in its fear and tumult and in facing mankind with fundamental issues – and Banquo, Donalbain and Malcolm are summoned from their beds as the dead will be called from their graves on the last day (74–9). This startling image has been prepared for by the Porter's fantasy of hell-gate and by Lennox's account of the natural and supernatural disturbances that show the universal significance of Duncan's murder as a violation of divine order (see page 4). Taken together these passages are reminiscent of mediaeval pictures of the Last Day in which bewildered spirits are led to judgement amid a disintegrating world filled with supernatural portents while devils, both comic and terrifying in their grotesqueness, wait at the mouth of hell to torment those who are damned.

The scene is one of confusion and uncertainty, alive with irony and innuendo. Macduff cannot know how mistaken he is in addressing Lady Macbeth as 'gentle lady' and assuring her that

> The repetition in a woman's ear
> Would murder as it fell. (81–4)

Her response, 'What! in our house?' (86) is curiously inept: does Banquo imply a rebuke in his reply? Macbeth achieves a more convincing demonstration of grief (89–94), perhaps because this is what he really feels, though he does not know how completely his words will be proved true (see page 48). He has had the presence of mind to kill Duncan's attendants – apparently not a part of Lady Macbeth's plan – and uses his excuse for this impulsiveness as a further demonstration of his loyalty. The ornate imagery of Duncan's 'silver skin laced with his golden blood' (110) is in keeping with Macduff's description of the body as 'The Lord's anointed temple' – Duncan is being transformed into a saintly relic – and Macbeth's perception of each wound as 'a breach in nature' (111) again emphasises the magnitude of this violation of natural order. As the speech develops it might seem that his emotions are beginning to run away with him – we know that these could be his genuine feelings – and this may be the explanation of Lady Macbeth's fainting; fearing that he will unintentionally betray them she creates a diversion. Her faint may, however, be genuine, and the first sign of the weakening that leads to her collapse at the end of the play. She, too, has had to screw up her courage both to go through with the murder and to master her husband's weakness, and when she is able to relax she might well give way completely.

The reactions of the thanes is varied. Lennox reports only that 'Those of his chamber, as it seemed, had done't', although he seems impressed by the circumstantial evidence (99–103); but Macduff's question about their killing (105) is direct and even challenging. Macbeth would be particularly watching Banquo, especially when he proposes that they 'question this most bloody piece of work' (126). It is Banquo who takes control of the situation, and his firm statement of loyalty (128–30) is the one stable point amidst the general confusion. The 'Fears and scruples' to which he refers are clearly shown in the tense interchanges between Malcolm and Donalbain. They realise that they would be the next target for the murderer (137–41) and Malcolm shows that not everyone is taken in by elaborate expressions of grief (134–5). The wisdom and morality of their flight has been questioned: they are deserting Scotland and playing into the hands of the murderer by leaving no other claimant to the throne and casting suspicion on themselves (II.iv.25–7); but they are young (IV.iii.14) and this moral uncertainty is typical of the conditions produced by acts of tyranny, as Ross later describes them (IV.ii.18–22).

Act II, Scene iv

Ross and an Old Man describe the strange disturbances that are occurring in the natural world. Macduff enters and tells them that because of their flight Malcolm and Donalbain are suspected of having bribed Duncan's attendants to murder him, that Macbeth is to be crowned at Scone, and that Duncan has been buried at Colme-kill. Macduff will not attend the coronation.

This is a choric scene (see page 63), in which the characters comment on the events of the play and supply information about their further development. The Old Man's long experience gives authority to his opinions, and as he has no distinctive rank he speaks as a representative of the ordinary people.

Darkness continues to shroud the earth, excluding the life-giving light (6–10); it is described in terms of the anger of the heavens to continue the suggestion of divine judgement hanging over the murder of Duncan. 'Act' and 'stage' (5–6) suggest a theatrical image, and the canopy, painted with signs of the zodiac, that extended over the Jacobean stage was called the 'heavens'; Shakespeare is thus involving the actual structure of his stage in the religious symbolism of the play. The inversions of natural order described by Ross and the Old Man (see pages 4–5) emphasise the unnaturalness of the murder, and as the stability of nature depends on its order an act that violates it is self-destructive (see page 59); as Ross says of the supposed guilt of Duncan's sons, by murdering their father they have not only rebelled against the natural hierarchy of the family but also destroyed the source of their own existence (27–9).

Ross doubtless represents the Scottish nobility in accepting the guilt of Malcolm and Donalbain and the inevitability of Macbeth's accession to the throne. Macduff is also prepared to report the general opinion without comment, although with a hint of irony when he recalls how Macbeth had destroyed the crucial evidence (23), but his decision not to attend the coronation shows that his question to Macbeth about his killing of the grooms (II.iii.105) was prompted by deep suspicion. The respect for the royal house that he showed after the murder of Duncan is reinforced here by the reverence with which he speaks of its ancestral tombs (33–5), and he fears that Macbeth's reign will be less easy than that of his predecessor, although this, too, he expresses with guarded irony through a significant extension of the metaphor of clothing (see page 12).

Act III, Scene i

Banquo is convinced that Macbeth gained the throne by evil means, but the fulfilment of the Witches' prophecies for Macbeth gives him hope that their promise to him will also be fulfilled. Macbeth and Lady Macbeth enter as king and queen, and Macbeth questions Banquo closely about his movements that day. Dismissing the court, he summons two men whom he has ordered to attend at the palace and while waiting for them reflects on his fear of Banquo and his frustration that it will be Banquo's descendants who will succeed to his throne. The men enter and he arranges for them to murder Banquo and Fleance.

The previous scene concluded with Macduff's suspicions about Macbeth; this one opens with Banquo's virtual certainty of his guilt. It is surprising, therefore, that he shows no signs of intending, or even wishing, to expose him. He is preoccupied instead with the thought that Macbeth's success augurs well for the fulfilment of the Witches' prophecy about his own descendants. The 'cursed thoughts' that they have prompted (II.i.8) may have found a weakness even in Banquo's moral armour, so that, while he would not consider any active evil, he is prepared to let things take their course – putting the interests of his own family above the immediate good of Scotland. It has been argued that there is no effective action he can take against Macbeth at this time, and that Jacobean political theory was reluctant to approve of rebellion even against a usurper once he had been crowned (see page 4), but Macbeth is not only a usurper but the murderer of a particularly saintly king. These explanations might serve as excuses for Banquo's inaction, but one must be struck by the contrast between his profession of absolute loyalty to Macbeth (15-18) and Macduff's honest refusal to attend his coronation, even though he has less reason for his suspicions.

Having achieved the throne Macbeth has gained in assurance and in low cunning. He and Lady Macbeth treat Banquo with particular respect, and while he slips in casual questions to learn when Banquo will return to the palace and whether Fleance will accompany him (19, 23, 35) he seeks to lull any suspicion of his intention by emphasising his wish to have the benefit of Banquo's counsel the following day (20-2, 32-4) and to see him at the banquet that evening (11-15, 27) – with devastating ironic effect when Banquo does attend it. Banquo's replies are characteristically open and guileless, apparently with no thought that Macbeth might have designs against the only witness of his meeting with the Witches.

Against the less favourable impression of Banquo at the beginning of the scene must be balanced Macbeth's unwilling tribute to his character (48-56), the more impressive in coming from his intended murderer. The 'royalty' of his nature arises from the harmonious balance of his faculties, the proper subordination of his courage to his wisdom (52-3; see page 5). He is not mastered by a dominating passion or rent by conflicting impulses; he exercises a regal control over his desires and actions. He is the antithesis to Macbeth, an integrated personality, always in command of himself, which is why Macbeth feels inferior in his presence and his 'Genius' – his guardian spirit – is cowed by that of Banquo. It is for this as much as for fear of anything that Banquo might do that he wants him killed. It blinds him to the irrationality of his intention: as he trusted the Witches' prophecies for himself he has no reason to hope that he can thwart their prophecy to Banquo – the 'fate' that he calls to support him (70-1) must oppose him – and as they had prophesied that Banquo's descendants would be kings but not Banquo himself Macbeth is really safer with Banquo alive than with him dead. But he cannot bear the contrast between the fertility promised to Banquo, as father of a line of kings, and the barrenness of his own reign. This contrast between their future destinies is an external expression of the difference between their characters. Macbeth is already beginning to realise how sterile his triumph has been. He has the title of king, but it is Banquo who is royal in himself, and it was the means that he adopted to obtain that title that destroyed the potential royalty in his own nature – defiled his character, banished his peace of mind and sacrificed his immortal soul (63-8). He still refers to Duncan as 'gracious' (65), but this no longer excites agonies of conscience, only the wish to destroy whatever reminds him of the graces he has sacrificed.

Macbeth's handling of the men he has chosen to murder Banquo shows how low he has sunk; he tends to bluster. They have met with ill fortune and at an earlier meeting he had tried to persuade them that it was Banquo who had oppressed them, not himself, as they had believed – the implication is that their belief was in fact correct. The hectoring tone with which he summarises this (76-83) betrays his insincerity, and even the potential murderers seem unimpressed. The laconic 'You made it known to us' (83) is equivalent to 'So you told us', with the implication that they have no interest in whether or not it is true. Macbeth continues with a heavily sarcastic dismissal of Christian forgiveness (85-90) and a pretentious discourse on the relative values and status of different breeds of dog and types of men; this depends, ironically, on the principle of hierarchy that he has violated – and continues to violate as he concludes, like Lady Macbeth (I.vii.49-51), that it is a readiness to murder that proves one is 'Not i' the worst rank of manhood' (102). The reply (107-13) shows that all this is hardly necessary; they are so desperate that they will do anything to improve their fortunes, or 'spite the world'. Macbeth seems to derive satisfaction from manipulating these seedy characters, like a cheap gangster, and in forcing them to acquiesce in his unconvincing justification of the murder, but once they have agreed to it he loses interest. When the First

Murderer tries to enter into the spirit of the game with a heroic declaration of loyalty (126) he cuts him off with the sardonic, 'Your spirits shine through you', tells them that they will receive precise instructions and dismisses them with the injunction that he wants a clean job, Fleance must be killed as well as Banquo. The scene concludes with a cynical couplet parallel to that with which Macbeth had set out for Duncan's chamber.

Act III, Scene ii

Both Lady Macbeth and Macbeth are oppressed by thoughts of their insecurity. Lady Macbeth urges her husband to put on a cheerful appearance for the coming banquet and he tells her to express particular esteem for Banquo. When she hints that Banquo and Fleance can be murdered he informs her that a dreadful deed will be committed that evening but not what it will be.

The disillusionment of Macbeth and Lady Macbeth emerges openly in this scene. She chides her husband for keeping alone (8), but the only encouragement she can offer is,

> Things without all remedy
> Should be without regard; what's done is done. (11–12)

The last statement recalls Macbeth's soliloquy, 'If it were done, when 'tis done', but there is a significant change of tone. There is no satisfaction in the completion of their enterprise, only a grim resignation, and 'Things without all remedy' suggests that a remedy would be welcome if one were available. Her own solitary thoughts take a similar form to his; lines 6–7 exactly parallel lines 19–26 in meaning, but her statement is terse and matter-of-fact, confined within its couplet, while his is impassioned. Her subdued 'dwell in doubtful joy' is replaced by the agonizing image of the mental rack on which Macbeth suffers 'In restless ecstasy'. His pun on 'peace' points the irony that their efforts to ensure their own peace have only succeeded in destroying it; and while she recognises that it is 'safer to be that which we destroy', much more genuine feeling is expressed by the way in which he lingers for four lines over the peace that Duncan enjoys (23–6). The intensity of Macbeth's speech shows that it is not only the insecurity of their position that torments them; he refers to 'these terrible dreams That shake us nightly' (18–19) – since he had murdered sleep (II.ii.36) – and his frustration that their efforts should have produced only the reverse of what was intended is creating a new mood of desperate ruthlessness. If necessary he will carry his revolt against natural order to the extreme: 'let the frame of things disjoint, both the worlds suffer' (16).

The remainder of the scene, the prelude to the murder of Banquo, is almost a re-enactment of the preparations for the murder of Duncan, emphasising their inability to escape from the world of deception and darkness once they have entered it. There is the same need for disguise (compare I.v.62–5, 70–2; vii.81–2), although now what they had thought a temporary expedient has to become a settled habit:

> Unsafe the while, that we
> Must lave our honours in these flattering streams,
> And make our faces vizards to our hearts. (32–4)

Macbeth's address to night (46–53), with its natural denizens – the bat, the 'shard-borne beetle' (40–2) – and its 'black agents' (53), closely parallels their previous invocations (I.iv.50–3, v.49–53). Their initial evil has committed them to a life of evil, and Macbeth's final couplet (54–5) shows that he has come to accept this as a general truth.

There is one striking difference, it is now Macbeth who takes the lead. His wife still chides him (8–12, 35), but while she suggests the murder of Banquo and Fleance (38), he has anticipated her, and does not even tell her what is planned. 'Be innocent of the knowledge, dearest chuck' (45), with its familiar endearment, even implies that she must be protected from the knowledge, that she is lapsing, or being pushed back, into the passive feminine role that she had contemptuously rejected.

Act III, Scene iii

The two murderers lying in wait for Banquo are joined by a third sent by Macbeth. Banquo is killed, but Fleance escapes.

The murder of Banquo is treated economically. The conclusion of the previous scene has provided an ominous setting, which is supplemented by the First Murderer as the light begins to fade (5–8), and Banquo's casual comment on the weather gives a final glimpse of his unsuspicious nature before the First Murderer's sardonic reply gives the signal for the blows to rain down (16).

The appearance of the Third Murderer cannot be conclusively explained. It is generally accepted that he has been sent by Macbeth to ensure that the first two do not betray him, illustrating a tyrant's inability to trust anyone. On the other hand, an audience hearing

> he delivers
> Our offices, and what we have to do,
> To the direction just (2–4)

might well assume that he had brought the more precise information that Macbeth had promised the other two (III.i.127–131). The fact that the Second Murderer says this to show that the Third can be trusted, and so must already know Macbeth's intentions in order to judge that the Third has not misinterpreted them, does not necessarily disprove this as it might mean only that the Third Murderer's detailed instructions agreed with the general plan that Macbeth had outlined to them. The escape of Fleance seems to have been helped by the extinguishing of the light, so it may be relevant that it is the Third Murderer who asks, 'Who did strike out the light?' and the First replies, 'Was't not the way?' (19), indicating either that it was the First who bungled things and the Third who was more adequately briefed, or that there was a lack of understanding between the Third and the other two so that it was Macbeth's additional precaution in sending him that led to the murder being botched.

Act III, Scene iv

As the thanes gather for the banquet Macbeth mingles hospitably with them while Lady Mabeth remains apart. The First Murderer, unseen by all but Macbeth, reports their limited success; Macbeth is temporarily dismayed by Fleance's escape, but takes heart from the death of Banquo. Lady Macbeth recalls him to his duty as host and as he expresses regret at Banquo's absence his ghost enters and sits in Macbeth's place. Macbeth is unable to conceal his horror, but when he recovers and challenges it the ghost disappears. Attempting to excuse his behaviour, he drinks to Banquo and the ghost again enters. He recovers more quickly this time and the ghost departs when he orders it to. The suspicions of the thanes are now aroused and Lady Macbeth, who has been trying to save the situation, dismisses them hastily. Macbeth resolves to maintain his throne by increasingly desperate measures; he plans to follow up Macduff's reported refusal to attend the court and to compel the Witches to tell him more.

This scene is the turning point of the play. It concludes its first half, concerned with Macbeth's rise to power, by showing him in regal state entertaining his thanes, and initiates the second movement, the counter-action against Macbeth, by providing the occasion for him to betray himself to the court. There is no doubt that the thanes have heard enough to be convinced of his guilt, and III.vi confirms that Lennox's parting words (119-20) are ironic.

Banqueting is a powerful symbol in the play, combining eating, the basic activity for the maintenance of life and health, with human fellowship. Macbeth has already been separated from his fellow men by his guilty thoughts at the banquet he gave for Duncan, and now, ironically, it is the murder of Banquo, which was intended to enable them to eat their meals without fear (III.ii.17), that precipitates his final alienation from human society. A banquet is also an ordered festivity, symbolising the harmonious order in the state. The thanes sit according to their ranks – Macbeth's first words are, 'You know your own degrees, sit down' – and Lady Macbeth reminds him that 'the sauce to meat is ceremony' (35), formal, courteous hospitality. As Macbeth has disrupted the moral and political order, so he now disrupts the feasting 'With most admired disorder' (109) and the banquet which began with a proper regard for precedence concludes with Lady Macbeth's hasty injunction

> Stand not upon the order of your going,
> But go at once. (118-19)

The hinge on which the plot turns is Banquo, and his contribution is profoundly ironic. While in life he has failed to expose Macbeth, he fulfils that duty by his death. The irony is pointed by Macbeth's anxiety that he should fall into the trap prepared for his return to the palace – 'Fail not our feast' he urges him with hypocritical hospitality (III.i.27); Banquo does not fail it, and Macbeth is caught in the unexpected consequences of the trap that he has himself laid.

The ghost may be an actual ghost or another hallucination, such as the 'air-drawn dagger' (61) to which Lady Macbeth compares it. Only Macbeth sees it, but this is not conclusive as ghosts were sometimes seen only by the person with whom they were directly concerned: the ghost of Hamlet's father, for example, is seen by everyone present at the beginning of the play, but only by Hamlet on its third appearance. More significantly, the ghost appears only when Macbeth is thinking of Banquo, when, ironically, he is expressing a wish that Banquo were present – presenting him with 'eminence' (III.ii.31) to allay any suspicion of his complicity in the murder. It disappears when he gets a grip on himself and challenges it (69-72) or orders it to go (105-6). Its appearance and disappearance depends on the state of Macbeth's mind, although even this is not entirely conclusive as the appearance of an actual ghost might be determined by the thoughts of the person to whom it was to show itself. In some productions no ghost appears on the stage and Macbeth addresses an empty seat; in others Banquo enters as a ghost, either because the ghost is being presented as really existing, or because the scene is being shown through Macbeth's eyes. Its appearance, whether seen by the audience or only described by Macbeth's words, is ghastly – with fixed, glaring eyes (94-5) and 'twenty mortal murders' on its crown (80), nodding and shaking its gory locks in insistent, dumb accusation (69, 49-50).

The scene is also the turning point for the characters. At the start Lady Macbeth has the more subdued manner that appeared in the previous scene. She is somewhat withdrawn, she 'keeps her state' (5), but she is alert to any signs of weakness in her husband (31-6) and when he is overwhelmed by the appearance of the ghost she rises superbly to the crisis, attempting to shame him by the familiar appeals to his manhood (57, 72-3) and offering excuses to their guests (52-7, 95-7). When she finally takes control of the situation and dismisses them she still preserves the pretence of social life – 'A kind good night to all' (120) – even though the cause is clearly lost. But this is the last time in the play that we see her asserting herself, and at the end of the scene she seems exhausted, offering no opinion about Macduff but merely asking submissively, 'Did you send to him, sir?' (128). Instead of rebuking Macbeth for his behaviour she wearily consoles him, 'You lack the season of all natures, sleep' (140), and these are the last words we hear from her before her sleep-walking scene.

The progress of Macbeth's character is in the opposite direction. This is the last occasion on which he is overcome by guilt – the last, if the ghost is a hallucination, on which his conscience projects accusing images through his imagination – and this time the loss of control is only temporary. At the first appearance of the ghost he betrays his guilt, protesting feebly that it was not he who did the actual killing (49–50), but instead of collapsing into abject self-condemnation as he did after the murder of Duncan he is now able to brace himself to face these horrors, defying the unspoken accusation – 'If thou canst nod, speak too' (69). The decisive moment comes perhaps with the sudden realisation expressed in 'Why, what care I!' that prefaces this challenge. Henceforth his speeches have a savage reckless-ness even before the thanes have left. He still fears the apparition – it is 'more strange Than such a murder is' (81–2) – but he can reduce the murder itself to its brutal physical facts,

> The time has been
> That when the brains were out the man would die,
> And there an end; (77–9)

this simple expression of his desperate wish that 'it were done, when 'tis done' (I.vii.1) is almost comic in its frustration. When he finally dismisses the ghost, and with it the last outward expression of his conscience, both have become an 'Unreal mockery' (106); he has achieved the hardened cynicism for which he has striven, and can claim, from the narrow stand-point to which he is now reduced, 'I am a man again' (107).

By the end of the scene it seems that physical courage is all that is left of his earlier nobility. He recognises that he cannot avoid exposure (121–5) – 'blood will have blood' recalls his earlier fear that he would merely be teaching 'Bloody instructions' (I.vii.9) – but this induces only a weary determination to pursue the course to which he is committed:

> I am in blood
> Stepp'd in so far that, should I wade no more,
> Returning were as tedious as go o'er. (135–7)

The self-accusations of his conscience are belittled as a 'self-abuse'; and he determines to bludgeon it into insensibility by 'hard use', adding grimly, 'We are yet but young in deed' (142–3).

His decision to seek out the Witches also shows the decisive change that has taken place. His first meeting with them had been unsought, but now it is he who approaches them, with no attempt to conceal from himself the nature of the evil he is embracing,

> for now I am bent to know
> By the worst means the worst. (133–4)

'All causes shall give way' for his own 'good' (134–5); evil has become his good. His attitude is that of Lady Macbeth when she deliberately summoned the 'murdering ministers' (I.v.47) and he no longer needs her to strengthen his resolution. It may be her recognition of this that contributes to her collapse at the end of the play, now that she does not have to brace her own will to counter his weakness.

In constructing this scene as the pivot at the mid-point of the action Shakespeare contrives one of the most audacious manipulations of time within his plays. The banquet takes place soon after Duncan's murder – news has only recently arrived of the whereabouts of Malcolm and Donalbain (III.i.29–32) – and at the beginning Macbeth is still ingratiating himself with his thanes. By the end, however, Macbeth has become a complete tyrant, with a network of spies throughout his kingdom (130–1), and by III.vi and IV.ii, which must follow soon after, the whole of Scotland is groaning under his rule. Developments that must have taken a considerable time are compressed into a single scene, but the concentration on Macbeth's psychological transformation is so intense that an audience is not aware of any improbability.

Act III, Scene v

Hecate rebukes the Witches for having dealings with Macbeth without consulting her and orders them to prepare charms to further their deception of him.

This scene and lines 39–43 and 125–32 of IV.i, are almost certainly not by Shakespeare. They are written in tetrameter verse (see page 9) which is almost invariably used for the Witches in the play; but instead of a forceful trochaic beat they have an iambic rhythm, with the accent on the second syllable, which gives them a light, tripping movement. The music and songs in this scene and at IV.i.43, are equally inappropriate for Shakespeare's 'secret, black, and midnight hags' (IV.i.48). The songs are in fact taken from Thomas Middleton's play *The Witch*, and were probably added, with this scene, because of the popularity of the Witches in the play. Hecate contributes nothing to the action, although her conclusion,

> security
> Is mortals' chiefest enemy, (32–3)

accurately describes the purpose of the apparitions, which contribute to Macbeth's fall by giving him a false sense of security.

Act III, Scene vi

Lennox shows that Macbeth's guilt has been widely recognised. The Lord informs him that Macduff has rebuffed Macbeth's messenger and has gone to the English court, where Malcolm has taken refuge, to request the help of Siward, Earl of Northumberland, to rid Scotland of tyranny.

Like II.iv this is a choric scene; the anonymous Lord is representative of the Scottish nobles as the Old Man represented the common people. The knowledge of Macbeth's crimes is being spread throughout the nobility.

Lennox's speech is ironic throughout, matching his sardonic farewell to Lady Macbeth at the end of III.iv. This indirectness may be prompted by caution - his 'former speeches' to the Lord seem to have been considerably more guarded (1-2), and he breaks off with the warning that 'broad words' have contributed to Macduff's disgrace (21-3) - but he makes his meaning clear in the parenthesis (19).

Macbeth's tyranny is now widespread and is described in terms of two of the basic symbols of the play when the Lord hopes that

> we may again
> Give to our tables meat, sleep to our nights,
> Free from our feasts and banquest bloody knives; (33-5)

it is as if the afflictions that plague Macbeth have infected his kingdom. In contrast, the sanctity of the English King is emphasised (30), and both the Lord and Lennox hope for divine aid to free their country from the tyrant (32-3, 45-9).

It might be more appropriate for this scene to follow IV.i: at the end of III.iv Macbeth decided to visit the Witches on the following day and at the same time to send the messenger to Macduff, thus the Lord could not know of the reception of the messenger until after Macbeth's meeting with the Witches in IV.i. It may have been moved to separate the two witch scenes when III.v was added. If it originally followed IV.i Lennox, of course, would have known of the flight of Macduff (IV.i.141-2) before the Lord tells him, but the role of Lennox in that scene, as a humble attendant on Macbeth, is incongruous however the scenes are arranged, and the more so if it follows his ironic exposure of Macbeth in III.vi. The explanation may be merely that someone was needed to bring Macbeth the news of Macduff's flight and Lennox, or the actor playing him, served the purpose.

Act IV, Scene i

The Witches prepare a charm by which they raise three Apparitions to answer Macbeth's unspoken questions: an armed head that warns him to beware of Macduff; a bloody child that tells him that no one born of woman shall harm him; and a child crowned, with a tree in his hand, that promises that he shall not be vanquished until Birnam wood comes to

Dunsinane hill. Reassured, Macbeth insists on knowing whether Banquo's descendants will reign in Scotland and is shown a pageant of eight kings, the last holding a glass which shows the images of more kings, followed by Banquo who indicates that they are descended from him. The Witches vanish and Lennox enters with the news that Macduff has fled to England; Macbeth determines to massacre his family.

The Witches' charm is a concoction of fragments of creatures, indicating the antipathy of their practices to natural organic life (see pages 5-6). The creatures from which the ingredients are torn were thought to be either dangerous or malign, and the Turk, Tartar and 'blaspheming Jew' are included because of their hostility to Christianity. The preparation of the charm takes the form of an incantation and the magic number three is much in evidence: the brindled cat – one of the familiars – mews thrice to signal when they should begin (1); the incantation is divided into three parts by the refrain; there were nine pigs in the sow's litter (64-5); the Witches produce threefold replies when they speak in succession (61, 107-9); and the first two Apparitions repeat Macbeth's name three times (71,77).

Macbeth's first speech (50-61) also has the repetitive form of an incantation, and its content identifies him with the Witches' negative principles – a catalogue of disasters culminating in the total confusion of all nature's seeds and embryos (compare III.ii.16). He fancies he is conjuring the Witches by their own black arts, 'that which you profess' (50) – conjuring being the use of magical practices to raise and control spirits – but he is again deceived. His conjuring only shows he has accepted their doctrine of evil and is therefore ready to be further misled by the charm they have already prepared. He cannot even question, much less command, the Apparitions (70, 75), and their knowledge of his thoughts (69) shows the evil sympathy that must exist between the instruments of darkness and their victim.

The Apparitions deceive Macbeth with their words, but the forms they take reflect the true meaning of their messages. Macbeth probably assumes the armed head to be Macduff's, but at the end of the play it is ius own head that is severed from his body. The bloody child that prophesies that he will be killed by none of woman born represents the blood-stained infant, not born but delivered surgically, who has survived to kill Macbeth. The child crowned, with a tree in his hand, represents Malcolm, the young heir to the throne, carrying one of the branches from Birnam wood by which the prophecy will be unexpectedly fulfilled. These symbolic meanings are too obscure for Macbeth to recognise them without the benefit of hindsight, but he leaps to the more obvious, but incorrect, conclusions the more readily because they are what he wants to hear; as the First Apparition harped his fear aright (74), so the other two echo his hopes. Throughout he displays a heady confidence, treating the Apparitions with arrogant familiarity – 'Call 'em, let me see 'em' (63) – and making an off-hand jest about their ritual address to him (78). His increasing elation is in frightening contrast to their cold, sardonic control.

He still seems to think that he can control the Witches (104–5), and probably demands that they answer his question about Banquo's descendants in a desperate hope that they will change their original prediction (see III.i.70–1 and page 30), but in spite of their apparent reluctance to reveal it the show of kings must have been part of the Witches' intention; they know Macbeth's thoughts and have already prepared the charm that will answer his final question. Thus when he insists on being shown what will fill him with despair they comply, and exult in his anguish. The splendid royal pageant sweeps on to the stage showing Macbeth that he cannot alter fate, and 'the blood-boltered Banquo' smiles in triumph (123) to demonstrate the futility of his bloody deeds. The representation of the eight Stuart kings (see page 3) would have bridged the centuries between the reign of Macbeth and that of James I and given the play a startling contemporary relevance for its original audiences.

Macbeth can only curse the Witches and damn 'all those that trust them' (139), which, of course, includes himself. With the warning of the First Apparition confirmed by the flight of Macduff (142), and unable to eliminate Banquo's descendants, he resolves to destroy Macduff's. To call this pointless decision one of the 'firstlings' (first-born children) of his heart (147) is savagely ironic, a perversion of the ideas of birth and childhood, and it is against birth and childhood that he is now striking. Obsessed by the sterility of his own reign his only relief is in equally sterile action, action that cuts off any further thinking – 'be it thought and done' (149) – but there is a shudder of horror in his last words before turning to Lennox – 'But no more sights!' (155).

Act IV, Scene ii
Lady Macduff is distressed by her husband's flight and Ross tries to persuade her that Macduff would have acted for the best. Her conversation with her son is interrupted by the hasty arrival of a stranger who warns her to flee, and he is followed immediately by Macbeth's agents who murder her and her son.

The violence of Lady Macduff's accusations against her husband arises from her sense of helplessness. She does not know why Macduff has gone to England and even when one knows his motive (III.vi.29–37) it might seem ill-advised to have left his family unprotected. He may not have imagined that even Macbeth would behave so savagely, and one can only accept Ross's assurance that he is the best judge in a situation fraught with danger and uncertainty. Ross gives a vivid picture of the effects of tyranny (17–22), when men may be declared traitors at the tyrant's whim, and alarming rumours proliferate in an atmosphere of fear even though no one knows what is to be feared; there is a constant flux of uncertainty and apprehension.

Lady Macduff turns sadly to her son for relief, giving wry expression to her sense of betrayal by her bantering remarks (30, 45) which she knows he will not take seriously. He diverts her with his childish knowingness and simple logic, which she encourages with mock gravity, but there is an uneasy contrast between his innocent assurance and her suppressed apprehension. The playful, inconsequential nature of their talk makes the sudden intrusion of the reality of Macbeth's Scotland the more shocking.

The messenger adds to the poignancy by his readiness to risk his life – he knows the murderers are hot on his heels – even though he is a stranger to Lady Macduff. When the murderers burst in, her defiant reply (80-1) to the question, 'Where is your husband?' shows her real feelings about him, and is matched by her son's response to the charge that his father is a traitor (82-3), a pathetic reminder of the earlier playful chatter about traitors (44-57).

The scene emphasises the unnaturalness of Macbeth's crimes; the murderer uses two of the play's most striking images of fertility and young life as terms of abuse, 'you egg! Young fry of treachery!' (82-3). The natural family loyalties it portrays are typified by 'the poor wren' that

<blockquote>
will fight,
Her young ones in her nest, against the owl (9-11)
</blockquote>

– one recalls the owl that screamed when Duncan was murdered – and the comparison with the world of nature is continued when the son says that he will live 'As birds do' (32), but his mother's sad reflection,

<blockquote>
Poor bird, thou'dst never fear the net nor lime,
The pitfall nor the gin, (34-5)
</blockquote>

is proved true when his confident 'Poor birds they are not set for' (36) is brutally contradicted, emphasising the pointlessness of this murder.

Act IV, Scene iii

Macduff has arrive at the English court to persuade Malcolm to return to Scotland to overthrow Macbeth. Malcolm fears that Macduff may intend to betray him to Macbeth and tests him by declaring that he would be an even worse tyrant. When Macduff gives up his attempt in despair Malcolm is satisfied that he is not merely trying to lure him into Macbeth's power; he takes back the slanderous account he has given of himself and tells Macduff that he is about to set out for Scotland for Siward and ten thousand men. Ross enters with further news of Scotland and eventually brings himself to report the massacre of Macduff's family, which increases their determination to destroy the tyrant.

The scene opens with Malcolm's apparent despair, which must be feigned to conceal his actual intention (133–5), and Macduff's account of the evils afflicting Scotland. The progression from the Lord's largely metaphorical account of their sufferings – 'Give to our tables meat, sleep to our nights' (III.vi.34) – to Ross's description of the general state of apprehension (IV.ii.18–22), and now to Macduff's mention of actual atrocities,

> New widows howl, new orphans cry, new sorrows
> Strike heaven on the face, (5–6)

gives the audience the impression of rapidly increasing tyranny. We have just seen one such atrocity, of which Macduff is of course ignorant, and Malcolm's distrust of him is an example of the uncertainties described by Ross as sapping the morale of the tyrant's opponents.

So far we have seen little of Malcolm and not much more of Macduff; the latter's reverence for the anointed king and his resolute opposition to Macbeth have been emphasised, but the characters of both need to be developed for them to seem worthy antagonists of Macbeth. In II.iii Malcolm is shown to be cautious but capable of making quick decisions. He is wary of taking professions of sorrow at their face value (II.iii.134–5); like his father he knows that one cannot 'find the mind's construction in the face' (I.iv.11–12), but unlike Duncan (see page 14) he applies this knowledge in practice. Even Macbeth 'Was once thought honest' (13), so Macduff's reputation is no guarantee of his loyalty. Malcolm explains his caution with disarming frankness: Macduff was once a friend of Macbeth, Macbeth has not yet harmed him, Macduff might profit by betraying Malcolm (13–17) and, with bitter irony, Macdufff's readiness to leave his wife and children unprotected suggests he does not fear for their safety (26–8). His statement is judicious and balanced: he acknowledges that the treachery of one thane does not prove that all are treacherous – 'Angels are bright still, though the brightest fell' (22) – and he apologises to Macduff if he is misjudging him since his suspicions cannot alter Macduff's true character (20–1, 29–31). These intricate speeches tease out the problem of distinguishing reality from appearance that runs through the play, and this is carried further by the testing of Macduff.

The method Malcolm employs might seem artificial, but it serves the additional dramatic purpose of providing a general context for the presentation of Macbeth's tyranny, contrasting a comprehensive catalogue of the vices of a tyrant, all of which Malcolm pretends to have (57–90), with the virtues of an ideal monarch, the 'king-becoming graces' which he claims he has 'no relish of' (91–100). He would 'Pour the sweet milk of concord into hell', as Macbeth, now drained of 'th' milk of human kindness' (I.v.16), is spreading discord throughout Scotland. This contrast is the constant theme throughout this somewhat episodic scene. It is continued by Macduff's idealised description of the piety of Malcolm's parents (108-11), by Malcolm's account of his actual disposition (125-31), and by the description of the saintly English King, with his miraculous powers of healing and prophecy (141-59; see page 5).

This description of Edward the Confessor stands apart from the action of the play, embodying an ideal of kingship that informs much of the imagery in the later scenes. Only a legitimate king can cure the diseases and heal the wounds inflicted by tyranny. Malcolm says of Scotland that 'each new day a gash Is added to her wounds' (40-1), Macduff despairs of his country's ever seeing her 'wholesome days' again (105), and Malcolm tries to comfort Macduff by urging,

> Let's make us medicines of our great revenge
> To cure this deadly grief' (214-5)

the word 'grief' often being used for the pain of a wound. The contrast is taken to an extreme: Edward is presented as saintly, the tyrant as diabolical. He is 'Devilish Macbeth' (117) and 'this fiend of Scotland' (233); Macduff declares,

> Not in the legions
> Of horrid hell can come a devil more damned
> In evils to top Macbeth, (55-7)

and Malcolm's comparison of Macbeth's treachery to the fall of Lucifer (22) associates him with the prince of devils, Satan. Conversely, Malcolm's reference to himself as a 'weak, poor, innocent lamb' in danger of being sacrificed (16-17) may associate him with Christ, who is often symbolised as a lamb and his crucifixion as a sacrifice to redeem mankind. The association is only fragmentary, Malcolm is not a 'Christ figure', but there is no doubt of the sanctity of his mission, and he and his supporters become agents of divine justice as 'the powers above Put on their instruments' (238-9) at the end of the scene.

The focus returns abruptly to Scotland with the arrival of Ross and his description of its still more intense suffering (164-76). He has great difficulty in bringing himself to tell Macduff of his personal tragedy, and in the end it comes with a rush (204-5). In contrast to the eloquence with which he responded to the public tragedy of Duncan's murder this personal blow renders Macduff inarticulate, and his grief is all the stronger for being locked within himself:

> The grief that does not speak
> Whispers the o'er-fraught heart and bids it break. (209-10)

He is stunned, repeatedly questioning the facts - 'My children too?' 'My wife killed too?' (211, 213) - and overwhelmed by a sense of guilt that they were killed because of his opposition to Macbeth (224-7). To Malcolm's attempt to comfort him he replies with bitter terseness, 'He has no children' (216). Most critics assume, probably correctly, that this refers to Malcolm - having no children he cannot understand Macduff's feelings - but there has been so much stress on the barrenness of the Macbeths that the relevance of this statement to the murderer cannot be ignored, especially when it is followed by repeated emphasis on the fecundity of Macduff's family -

> All my pretty ones?
> Did you say all? - O hell-kite! - All?
> What, all my pretty chickens and their dam
> At one fell swoop? (216-9)

accompanied by those striking images from the animal world that have symbolised natural fertility throughout the play - the martlets (I.vi.4-10), the 'egg' and 'fry' associated with Macduff's son (IV.ii.82-3), the wren that Lady Macduff says will fight against the owl, 'Her young ones in her nest' (IV.ii.9-11). There is a pathetic parallel between this example which Lady Macduff uses to illustrate her husband's lack of natural feeling and his grief-stricken image of his 'chickens and their dam' destroyed by the kite. Macduff has 'the natural touch' (IV.ii.9), and with Banquo dead he takes his place in the symbolic pattern of the play as the antithesis to Macbeth's sterility. This symbolic role is extended when Malcolm urges him to 'Dispute it like a man' and he replies, 'But I must also feel it as a man' (221), a telling rejection of the perverted concept of manhood represented by Macbeth.

In the course of this scene Malcolm shows his fitness to be king by his prudence, piety and resolution, and Macduff emerges as the champion not only of legitimate monarchy but of the life-giving forces of nature and of manhood in its full sense, ready to confront Macbeth:

> Front to front
> Bring thou this fiend of Scotland and myself. (232-3)

The optimistic ring of Malcolm's final couplet reverses the weary resignation of that with which Macbeth faces the future after his first meeting with the Witches (I.iii.146-7).

Act V, Scene i
Lady Macbeth's Gentlewoman tells a Doctor of her mistress's actions while she is asleep, but refuses to report what she has heard her say. Lady Macbeth enters sleep-walking, trying to wash imaginary blood from her

hands and reliving in dream form the crimes that she and Macbeth have committed.

Lady Macbeth has sunk from the disillusionment of III.ii and her exhaustion at the end of III.iv to the verge of a complete breakdown; the report of her suicide at the end of the play (V.ix.36-7) is anticipated by the Doctor's concern that she should be deprived of anything by which she might harm herself (77). While Macbeth has hardened himself to repress his inner feelings, her psychological defences have weakened, although it is only in her sleep that she reveals this. For considerable passages of Acts I and II one was living within Macbeth's mind, and now for the first time one is let into the inner world of Lady Macbeth, of which there have previously been only fleeting glimpses, for example at the beginning of II.ii. She had despised his imagination, but now hers plagues her in her dreams - the 'terrible dreams' to which Macbeth referred (III.ii.18). The ironic reversal of her previous attitudes is precise: previously she had summoned darkness, now 'she has light by her continually' (22-23); she dismissed the imaginary voice that Macbeth heard crying 'Sleep no more' (II.ii.35), now she cannot rest - she had called his preoccupation with it 'brainsickly' (II.ii.46) but it is her mind that is 'infected' (73); she had told him, 'A little water clears us of this deed' (II.ii.67), now she cannot wash off the imaginary blood that symbolises her guilt (26-35, 50) -

> all the perfumes of Arabia will not sweeten this little
> hand (50-2)

is the exact equivalent of Macbeth's

> Will all great Neptune's ocean wash this blood
> Clean from my hand? No. . ., (II.ii.60-1)

and a very feminine equivalent for a woman who has tried to reject her feminine nature.

The nightmare world that Macbeth inhabits after the murder of Duncan (see page 23) comes to her nightly, but their imaginations operate very differently. Hers does not torment her with accusing voices or images of explicit moral condemnation. Though everything she says is full of despair and punctuated with sighs (52-6), there is only one specific expression of regret for their crimes - the plaintive 'The Thane of Fife had a wife; where is she now? (42-3) - and only one indication of any religious awareness, and that entirely negative, 'Hell is murky' (36). She is simply trapped in her past crimes, chiefly in the murder of Duncan, although Banquo is mentioned once (63-4) and Macbeth's 'flaws and starts' at the banquet (III.iv.62) may be recalled when she rebukes him for 'starting' (45). But one murder merges with another as she is condemned to relive them in fragmentary form. She is still chiding her husband - 'Fie, my lord, fie!

A soldier, and afeard?' (36-7); directing his actions - 'Wash your hands, put on your nightgown; look not so pale' (62-3); expressing her former ruthless confidence - 'What need we fear who knows it, when none can call our power to account?' (37-9; compare I.vii.77-79); and experiencing the physical horror of murder - 'Here's the smell of the blood still' (50).

> Yet who would have thought the old man to have had so
> much blood in him? (39-40)

shows the disgust she felt, but rigidly concealed, when she returned the daggers, but there is no sympathy here for Duncan; the remark is appalling in its detachment. The 'old man' is only a distasteful fact; she is still as cynically self-centred as she has ever been; what she regrets is her own pollution. She cannot escape from the world of darkness and blood that she created for herself, or from the narrow destructive outlook that she cultivated: 'What's done cannot be undone' (68). She again recalls Macbeth's 'If it were done, when 'tis done' (I.vii.1). Previously, 'what's done is done' (III.ii.12) implied that it was no longer worth thinking about; this new restatement, on the contrary, expresses her despairing recognition that it cannot be eradicated, either from the record of the past or from her own mind. She has discovered that 'Things without all remedy' cannot 'be without regard' (III.ii.11-12). One can only regard her with a strange mixture of horror and pity.

As Macbeth's imagination forced him to betray himself at the banquet, so Lady Macbeth's dreams disclose her guilt, to the amazement of the Doctor. He is the counterpart to the English Doctor in the previous scene. The latter attests to the miraculous healing powers of the English King; the former diagnoses the incurable disease that afflicts the Scottish queen - it is beyond his practice (59). The unnaturalness of her mental troubles matches the unnaturalness of the deeds that have produced them (72-3): 'even-handed justice' has commended the ingredients of her poisoned chalice to her own lips (I.vii.10-12). He speaks in medical terms of her mind being 'infected', but indicates the spiritual source of the infection when he adds 'More needs she the divine than the physician' (75).

Act V, Scene ii

The Scottish thanes are marching to meet Malcolm and the English army near Birnam wood. Many of Macbeth's forces are deserting him and he is desperately fortifying the castle of Dunsinane.

This scene (like V.iv and V.vi) is brief and businesslike, reflecting the determination and practical activity of the forces opposing Macbeth, in contrast to the conditions within the castle of Dunsinane portrayed in the scenes that alternate with them. The colours and the regular drum beats convey their high morale and good military order. Previously Lady Macbeth was the efficient organiser; now while she is sunk in neurotic brooding Macbeth alternates between furious activity and gloomy meditation. Like her, although with different symptoms, he is losing self-control - 'Some say he's mad' (13) - as a result of his internal conflict -

> When all that is within him does condemn
> Itself for being there. (24-5)

The scene brings together four of the major strands of imagery in the play - blood, clothing, disease, and natural growth - and intertwines them in a complex commentary on the action. The image implied in Angus's words,

> Now does he feel
> His secret murders sticking on his hands, (16-17)

suggests that, again like his wife, Macbeth is unable to wash the symbolic blood from his hands, as he had feared after the murder of Duncan (II.ii. 60-3). Earlier still he had recognised that his 'Bloody instructions' would 'return To plague th' inventor' (I.vii.9-10) and now as 'minutely revolts upbraid his faith-breach' (18) the disloyalty of his subjects is fair return for his own disloyalty. The imagery of clothing shows vividly how the title of king mocks the inadequacy of the man who holds it:

> Now does he feel his title
> Hang loose about him, like a giant's robe
> Upon a dwarfish thief. (20-22)

Macbeth's new robes do not sit easily (II.iv.38); instead of his royal dignities moulding themselves to his person (see I.iii.144-6) the reverse has happened; he has lost what 'royalty of nature' he had and shrivelled up within them - drained 'dry as hay' (I.iii.18). This image has a paradoxical relationship to that in the previous speech by Caithness:

> He cannot buckle his distempered cause
> Within the belt of rule, (15-16)

which portrays a Macbeth bursting out of his clothes. Angus describes the personal inadequacy of Macbeth; Caithness the frantic activity with which he tries to compensate for it. This is a complicated image: 'cause' refers primarily to his control over his kingdom, but it was also a medical term, and so refers as well to Macbeth's own condition; 'distempered' means 'disordered' with reference to his kingdom, and 'diseased' with reference to himself - in this case a dropsy-like disease making his body swell. The disorder within his kingdom is identified with that within his own constitution. The image of disease in Scotland emerges explicitly when Caithness calls Malcolm 'the medicine of the sickly weal' and refers to themselves as their 'country's purge' (27-8), which will expel the poison of tyranny from the body politic. 'Each drop of us' (29) - each drop of blood - suggests blood-letting, another way of purging the body. This is picked up by Lennox and transformed into an image of growth – 'To dew the sovereign flower' (30) - while the resurgence of natural vitality in Scotland is symbolised by the presence in Malcolm's army of Siward's son

> And many unrough youths that even now
> Protest their first of manhood. (10-11)

Act V, Scene iii

Furious at the desertion of his thanes, Macbeth reassures himself with the predictions of the Apparitions. When he is informed of the approach of the English army he insists on arming at once, but pauses to speak to the Doctor about Lady Macbeth's health.

Macbeth oscillates between 'valiant fury' (V.ii.14) when he thinks of his enemies and near despair when he considers himself and his own life. He dismisses his disloyal thanes with flamboyant gestures (1, 7-8) but the trite balance of the rhymed couplet,

> The mind I sway by and the heart I bear
> Shall never sag with doubt nor shake with fear, (9-10)

makes his defiance seem a rather artificial pose, and his frustration is expressed in the crude abuse with which he hinders the attempt of the frightened servant to report the appearance of the English army. He is trying to escape from his sense of failure by action, but he cannot focus on the action. He insists on arming before it is necessary (33), he fires off orders (35-6), and Seyton, his squire, has to try to put on his armour while Macbeth talks moodily to the doctor or gives peremptory orders; he apparently does not succeed as he is told to 'Pull't off' (54) and 'Bring it after me' (58).

The extent of the conflict within Macbeth is evident in the contradiction between all this frenetic activity and his melancholy conviction that he has 'lived long enough' (22); he is determined to preserve a life that he no longer thinks worth preserving. In contrast to the youth and vitality of Malcolm's forces, his

> way of life
> Is fall'n into the sere, the yellow leaf. (22-3)

His reflections on old age may help to suggest the passage of time but do not mean that Macbeth is old; he is looking into a future that will be a continuation of his present situation, as Angus has reported it (V.ii.19-22):

> And that which should accompany old age,
> As honour, love, obedience, troops of friends,
> I must not look to have; but, in their stead,
> Curses, not loud but deep, mouth-honour, breath,
> Which the poor heart would fain deny, and dare not. (24-8)

His thoughts of old age suggest the contrast with the aged Duncan, and the love and loyalty that surrounded him (I.iv.33-5). But now 'Renown and grace is dead', as Macbeth declared at the discovery of Duncan's murder, in his show of grief that ironically foreshadows the actual disillusionment he expresses here. 'I have lived long enough' repeats

> Had I but died an hour before this chance,
> I had lived a blessed time, (II.iii.89-90)

and the image of decay, 'the sere, the yellow leaf', duplicates that of the wine lees (II.iii.93-4).

Macbeth is not only isolated from his friends and subjects, he has become remote even from his wife. It is only at the end of the scene that he inquires about her health, although the Doctor has been present throughout, and the Doctor's cautious reply (37-9) plunges him into still more profound meditation on the nature of their troubles (39-45), the 'mind diseased', the 'rooted sorrow' - sorrow is all that grows strongly for the Macbeths. The grave rhythm, the hypnotic regularity of the lines and the brooding repetitions suggest that he is sunk in thought, but the only remedy he can consider is 'some sweet oblivious antidote', recalling his envy of the peace that Duncan enjoys in the oblivion of death (III.ii.22-6). He is thinking at least as much of himself as of his wife, as is implied in the Doctor's reply:

> Therein the patient
> Must minister to himself. (46-7)

But Macbeth is long past grappling with his spiritual ills; throwing 'physic' contemptuously away he escapes from the pain they cause by flinging himself into the 'oblivious antidote' of action (48-9), and when he returns to the theme, to make the familiar connection between the diseases of the body and those of the state, it is with much less honesty. He knows the 'disease' (51) that afflicts his land, the Doctor does not need to cast its water, but all he now demands is a purge to rid it of the English (55-6) - as the rebel thanes had seen themselves as a purge to rid Scotland of tyranny (V.ii.28).

After this moment of insight Macbeth relapses into his blind faith in the Apparitions,

> I will not be afraid of death and bane
> Till Birnam forest come to Dunsinane, (59–60)

the scene ending as it began. But it is the Doctor who has the final word; his concluding couplet chimes in with that of Macbeth, puncturing its bravado with his canny realism:

> Were I from Dunsinane away and clear,
> Profit again should hardly draw me here. (61–2)

His regard for profit might refer to the traditional tight-fistedness of the Scots – those who followed James to England were notorious for their self-seeking – but doctors had enjoyed an even longer reputation for avarice.

Act V, Scene iv
The Scottish thanes have joined Malcolm, who orders his soldiers to carry branches hewn from Birnam wood to conceal their numbers.

The scene shows the orderly advance of Malcolm's forces. His calm instructions contrast with Macbeth's impetuous orders, and the unity of the English and Scottish forces emphasises the increasing isolation of Macbeth (10–14). We are reminded of his confidence of withstanding a siege in Dunsinane (8–10), and at the same time Malcolm's order to his soliders (4–7) foreshadows the way in which this confidence will be destroyed. Malcolm displays a youthful optimism, while the more experienced Macduff and Siward recommend that they concentrate on the business in hand instead of speculating on the outcome of the battle; 'Industrious soldiership' (16) sounds thoroughly professional.

Act V, Scene v
Assured of the strength of his castle, Macbeth is defying his enemies when the news of Lady Macbeth's death prompts more pessimistic reflections. The report that Birnam wood is approaching shatters the confidence he derived from the Third Apparition's prediction and he orders his forces to arm and attack the enemy in open battle, resolved at least to die fighting.

Macbeth continues to alternate between hectic confidence and disillusionment. He bursts in, brushing aside the apprehensive cries of 'They come', challenging his opponents with 'banners on the outward walls', and deriding them with the strength of his castle. The cry from Lady Macbeth's apartments makes him reflect grimly on the change that has come over him, and the news of her death plunges him into a disillusioned meditation on the worthlessness of life as a whole, which absorbs any personal grief he may feel. (For a detailed examination of lines 7–28, see pages 69–72).

His response to the news of his wife's death is in striking contrast to the violence with which he reacts to the astounded sentry's report that Birnam wood – not the English army (V.iii.11–18) – is advancing on the castle. His instant, frantic wrath – 'Liar and slave!' (35) – is immediately quenched by the realisation of what this means to him –

> If thy speech be sooth,
> I care not if thou dost for me as much. (40–1)

For a moment his resolution falters as he takes in the full significance of 'th' equivocation of the fiend', spelling out the impossible fact, 'and now a wood Comes toward Dunsinane', and describing the equivocal nature of evil with uncompromising simplicity, 'That lies like truth' – that deceives with words that in their literal sense are true but in their real significance totally misleading. The prediction of the Third Apparition has been fulfilled, but in precisely the opposite sense to that which Macbeth expected.

The paradoxical effect is to drive him from the defences of his castle, the strength of which has been emphasised at the beginning of the scene and on two previous occasions (V.ii.12; iv.10). As Hecate says, if in words that Shakespeare did not write, 'security Is mortals' chiefest enemy' (III.v.32–3). Macbeth's sense of security has depended so much on the predictions of the Apparitions that when they begin to fail him everything seems lost; the physical security of Dunsinane is insignificant by comparison, and he flings it away in a surge of desperation,

> If this which he avouches does appear,
> There is nor flying hence, nor tarrying here. (47–8)

Moreover, his despair at the worthlessness of his reign, and of life as a whole – now reinforced as the last assurances in which he put his trust begin to crumble – makes him almost suicidal:

> I 'gin to be aweary of the sun,
> And wish th' estate o' the world were now undone. (49–50)

All that is left to him is his fighting instinct, 'At least we'll die with harness on our back' (52).

The first stage of the trap set by the Witches has been sprung, Its cunning is that it makes Macbeth destroy himself; the scene that begins with his confidence in the strength of his castle ends, ironically, with his abandoning it. It is he who is making the prophecies come true.

Act V, Scene vi

Malcolm orders his soldiers to throw down their boughs and prepare for battle.

This brief scene again emphasises order (6) and the determination of Malcolm's forces (7–10). The trumpets increase the excitement as the first sounds of conflict, the alarums, are heard off-stage.

Act V, Scene vii

Macbeth kills Siward's son, and when he has left the stage Macduff enters in search of him, hurrying off to where the fighting sounds fiercest in the hope of finding him there. Siward tells Malcolm that the castle has surrendered without a fight and that the victory is almost complete.

The alarums continue, punctuating the scene with bursts of warlike sound. Macbeth is still reassuring himself with the promise of the Second Apparition. Now that the Third has betrayed him he sounds at first as if he were half expecting to meet such an apparent impossibility (2-4), but after he has killed Siward's son his renewed confidence appears in the sardonic 'Thou wast born of woman' and the swaggering couplet that follows it (12-13). His encounter with Young Siward – it is again youth that he destroys – gives some impression on stage of the general conflict, but the focus is entirely on Macbeth. Macduff is intent only on killing the murderer of his family, and Macbeth is increasingly isolated as his castle surrenders and his soldiers desert to Malcolm (28-9).

In some editions V.vii and V.viii are regarded as one continuous scene, so that the last scene of the play becomes V.viii, but as the action moves to a different part of the field most editors separate them.

Act V, Scene viii

Macduff fights with Macbeth and in reply to Macbeth's boast that he cannot be killed by one born of woman tells him that he was not born but delivered surgically. Macbeth's courage falters, but rather than submit to Malcolm he resolves to fight to the death and is killed.

Macbeth is determined to continue his career of destruction to the end, in contrast to the austere Roman tradition for defeated generals to commit suicide (1-3). There is a poignant moment when, as Macduff's challenge continues his identification with the Devil, Macbeth's human nature suddenly surfaces, as he is faced with the man who 'loved him well' (IV.iii.13) and whom he has so wronged:

> But get thee back, my soul is too much charged
> With blood of thine already. (5-6)

He may be remembering the warning of the First Apparition to beware Macduff, but the feeling of guilt sounds genuine, and he shows no further reluctance to fight as he exults in the invulnerability promised by the Second Apparition (8-13). It is only when Macduff destroys this final illusion and Macbeth realises the full extent of their equivocation – that their predictions are true in a literal sense but false in the hopes they arouse – that his courage fails. Macduff's brief statement that he was 'from his mother's womb Untimely ripped' (15-16) is charged with meaning, recalling the figure of the Second Apparition, a bloody child, and still more powerfully the image of pity

> like a naked new-born babe,
> Striding the blast (I.vii.21–22)

that Macbeth had foreseen as the agent of retribution.

By making Macbeth build his confidence upon an illusion the Apparitions again contribute to his defeat since his courage collapses when the illusion fails him, it cows his 'better part of man' (18); even the limited qualities of manhood that Lady Macbeth could recognise are undermined. His sulkily blunt 'I'll not fight with thee' is totally unrealistic, he has no alternative, and when Macduff's taunts bring him back to the reality of what surrender would mean he summons up his ordinary human courage, now bereft of 'metaphysical aid' (I.v.28), and fights to the death, although he must now know that he is doomed. His realisation that this is what the apparitions were actually predicting may be decisive in his defeat, and he certainly fights under a weight of guilt that has been briefly glimpsed at the beginning of the scene.

The stage direction 'Exeunt, fighting' is appropriate as Macduff enters with Macbeth's head in the next scene. In the first edition of the play, however, the further stage direction was added, 'Re-enter fighting, and Macbeth is slain', perhaps to indicate the length and ferocity of the struggle.

Act V, Scene ix

Malcolm and his forces enter victoriously. Siward learns of his son's death, but is content that he died bravely. Macduff enters with Macbeth's head and, with the other thanes, hails Malcolm as King of Scotland. Malcolm creates them earls and prepares to restore order and justice to his kingdom.

The trumpets signal the end of the battle and greet Malcolm with a fanfare. The scene is a rather formal conclusion to the play, given human interest by Siward's reception of the news of his son's death; as the representative of a heroic age his only concern is that he had not turned his back in flight but died honourably, defending a righteous cause.

If the audience has not seen Macbeth killed on stage the entry of Macduff is highly dramatic, with the head probably carried on the end of a pike. It is appropriately Macduff who hails the legitimate king, and sees him encompassed by his 'kingdom's pearl' (22), the thanes surrounding him symbolically like the jewels set round the crown. When Malcolm rewards them by creating them earls he is fulfilling his father's promise when he was created Prince of Cumberland –

> signs of nobleness, like stars, shall shine
> On all deservers (I.iv.41–2)

– and also inaugurating the new order in Scotland, substituting for the looser relationship of thane to king the hierarchical order of the feudal system. Macbeth and Lady Macbeth are summarily dismissed as 'this dead butcher and his fiend-like queen' (35), and we learn incidentally that Lady Macbeth probably committed suicide. She has become so insignificant that the manner of her death does not need to be established, but there is a last telling stroke of irony as her 'self and violent hands' (36) recall Macbeth's hands after the murder of Duncan – 'Ha! they pluck out mine eyes (II.ii.59). The chaos of tyranny is over, and Malcolm looks forward to the time when the kingdom will again be in harmony with both the divine and the natural order: he speaks of what should be 'planted newly with the time' (31) – recalling Duncan's words to Macbeth, 'I have begun to plant thee' (I.iv.28) – and concludes the play by appealing to divine grace to assist him to perform what needs to be done 'in measure, time, and place' (39).

3 THEMES AND ISSUES

Macbeth is steeped in contemporary superstition, but it is not a play about the supernatural. A Jacobean audience might well have seen Macbeth and Lady Macbeth as victims of demonic possession: at different times both of them appear in trance-like states, no longer in control of themselves – Lady Macbeth when sleep-walking, Macbeth when he first hears the prophecy that he will be king and when he moves compulsively to murder Duncan as if under hypnotic control (see pages 11–12 and 22). His inability to pray (II.ii.28–9) was a familiar sign of possession, and the 'damned spot' that Lady Macbeth canot wash off her hands is the equivalent of the Devil's mark that was reputedly to be found on a witch; she actually demands the attributes of a witch when she invokes the 'spirits That tend on mortal thoughts' (I.v.39–49). But no familiars appear – one might say that she doesn't need any – and the spot is a blemish on her mind, not her body. Malcolm may be justified in calling her 'fiend-like' (V.ix.35), but not even Malcolm says that she is a fiend.

The play accepts contemporary popular beliefs but explores the psychological and spiritual basis of Jacobean demonology. There is constant interweaving of the supernatural and the psychological and a gradation from one to the other, from the 'air-drawn dagger', which is certainly a hallucination (II.i.47–9), through the ghost of Banquo, which may be either a real ghost or only a projection of Macbeth's guilt (see page 34), to the Witches and the Apparitions, which must have an existence independent of Macbeth, although the reality of the former is questioned in the play (I.iii.53–4, 79–85) and the latter have an intimate relation with Macbeth's mind, knowing his thoughts and echoing his fears (IV.i.69, 74). This ambiguity in the treatment of the supernatural enables a modern audience to respond to the power that it still exercises over our imagination while recognising it as a projection of the characters' inner lives. The 'spirits That tend on mortal thoughts' that Lady Macbeth summons to fill her 'top-full Of direst cruelty' are an external symbol of her own 'spirits' that she will pour into her husband's ear to prompt his murderous thoughts (I.v.25). Macbeth and Lady Macbeth remain free agents, as free as the passions and hidden fears that lie below the conscious level allow any human being to be free. The witches would have no influence over Macbeth if they did not find a corresponding evil in his mind; they do not compel him to murder Duncan, they only encourage his ambition and leave his imagination to do the rest. ———————— *fatal flaw*

Much of the most significant action of the play takes place within Macbeth's imagination; we are taken inside the mind of a murderer and see things through his eyes. This is essential for his role of tragic hero, for he is the only protagonist in Shakespeare's tragedies who might be regarded as a 'villain' rather than a 'hero'; at the end of the play no sympathy is expressed for him and there is no reference to the qualities that have been tragically sacrificed by his fall. Even the heroic qualities that he displays at the beginning of the play are of a limited kind. He is praised for his loyalty and service to Scotland, but from his first appearance it is clear that these virtues have already been undermined. He may be a courageous warrior, but he is still that at the end of the play when we are almost ready to acquiesce in Malcolm's dismissal of him as 'this dead butcher' (V.ix.35). We sympathise intensely with Macbeth not because of the qualities he displays in action, but because we are able to take part in his internal conflict: feel his horrified response to his own evil thoughts (I.iii.134–42), share the overwhelming spiritual insights that persuade him to proceed no further with the murder (I.vii.16–25), and experience his agonies of conscience after he has committed it. It is this that enables us to appreciate his potential nobility. It is only potential, as we have to glimpse it almost in spite of Macbeth. He is unwilling to admit it to himself, pretending to be concerned only with whether he could get away with murder, but it is the more impressive for the power with which his moral imagination erupts through this facade of tough-mindedness (see pages 18–19) and finally shatters it when he experiences the reality of murder.

3.1 RETRIBUTION

The tragedy is heightened by the fact that Macbeth already knew what the consequences of his crime would be, but chose to repress that knowledge. The play demonstrates the inevitability of retribution because the retribution is in the nature of the action itself. In order to bring himself to murder Duncan he has to distort his nature, and finds that he must live distorted for the rest of his life. He thought that by murder he could become a king; he finds he has become only a murderer. In order to achieve the crown he has to destroy everything in himself that would make it more than an empty symbol. He discovers that one cannot insulate onself from one's own actions; he had hoped that he might shut his eyes to the deed performed by his hands (I.iv.52), but finds after the murder of Duncan that his hands pluck out his eyes (II.ii.59). Actions become a part of oneself, as Macbeth finds 'His secret murders sticking on his hands' (V.ii.17) and Lady Macbeth cannot wash the blood off hers. The relation of action to character is an insistent theme throughout the play. That is why there is repeated reference to the nature of 'doing'. Macbeth hopes that the murder will be 'done, when 'tis done' (I.vii.1), and it is indeed 'done', but the meaning of the word changes in the course of the play as Lady Macbeth unconsciously echoes this phrase in 'what's done is done' and later 'What's done cannot be undone' (see pages 31 and 45); the murder is no longer 'over and done with' but 'done and irrevocable', it has become an indelible part of their characters. Macbeth's realisation comes earlier. There is a similar shift of meaning between his words as he goes to murder Duncan, anxious to get it over, 'I go, and it is done' (II.i.62), and the horrified finality of 'I have done the deed' (II.ii.14) on his return; and by the end of the scene his one wish is that it could be undone, 'Wake Duncan with thy knocking! I would thou couldst' (II.ii.74).

Both Macbeth and Lady Macbeth have to live with their past crimes, and that is their punishment. There is also the fear of discovery, but that is not the primary cause of their 'terrible dreams' (III.ii.18); when Macbeth says 'Our fears in Banquo Stick deep' he may fear what Banquo might do, but what he dwells on is his sense of moral inferiority (see pages 29-30). The nature of this retribution is most vividly exposed when we penetrate behind the consciousness of the characters. In the Sleep-Walking Scene there is only one expression of regret for their victims, although a haunting one, and that is for a murder in which Lady Macbeth took no part. She shows no fear of punishment on earth and her stark statement 'Hell is murky' (V.i.36) is less an expression of a fear of future punishment than a description of her present situation, enveloped in the darkness that she originally courted but that she now dreads (V.i.22-3). She is simply reliving the murders; her punishment is to be trapped eternally in the arid, cynical character of murderess. Macbeth is a most powerful imaginative expression of the theological principle that hell is not a place but a state of mind. Lady Macbeth's hell is the knowledge of herself; she had willed that her milk should be taken for gall (I.v.47), and now all she can taste is the bitterness. Gerard Manley Hopkins's sonnet beginning 'I wake and feel the fell of dark' could be describing her situation:

> I am gall, I am heartburn. God's most deep decree
> Bitter would have me taste: my taste was me;
>   . . .I see

> The lost [the damned] are like this, and their scourge to be
> As I am mine, their sweating selves; but worse.

Macbeth suffers in a similar hell of his own making. His entry into it is marked by the fanciful transformation of the porter of his own castle into the porter of Hell-gate; he himself says that he has given his 'eternal jewel' to 'the common enemy of man' (III.i.67-8), and in the later scenes of the play he is commonly referred to as 'devil', 'fiend' or 'hell-hound'. He is in hell as that condition is described by Marlowe's devil, Mephistophilis, in *Doctor Faustus*:

> Hell hath no limits, not is circumscribed
> In one self place; for where we are is hell,
> And where hell is, there must we ever be.

For Macbeth, at least, the murder of Duncan is an 'image' of the 'great doom' (II.iii.77), because it was then that he judged and damned himself, a damnation that is expressed in his absolute self-condemnation in the scene that follows the murder. He had been prepared to 'jump the life to come' (I.vii.7), but spiritual as well as secular punishment comes in this life as well. He is continually tormented by the consequences for himself of his actions against others; it is his inability to rid his hands of blood that condemns him to a life of murder. He deliberately separates himself from humankind by repressing his own 'milk of human kindness' (I.v.16) and then finds he cannot escape from this self-imposed isolation. He is deprived of human fellowship, deserted by his followers, estranged from his wife, and no longer looks to have

> that which should accompany old age,
> As honour, love, obedience, troops of friends. (V.iii.24-5)

He is acutely aware of what he has sacrificed by killing 'the gracious Duncan' (III.i.65), and the thought makes death seem a release – 'I have lived long enough' (V.iii.22). His 'wine of life is drawn' (II.iii.93) and the bitterness of the lees that are left to him corresponds to the bitterness of Lady Macbeth's gall. The counterpart to her sleep-walking, in showing how his personality and outlook have been distorted by the horrors he has created, is the passage beginning 'I have almost forgot the taste of fears' (V.v.9-28). The tone is different; we are not admitted directly into his unconscious mind as we are into Lady Macbeth's and his stern acceptance of a continuing familiarity with 'direness' and 'slaughterous thoughts' does not have the despairing pathos of his wife's reliving of those horrors, but the second of these two speeches (V.v.19-28) shows what this callousness has cost him, and reveals as profound a despair: the whole of life is only 'a tale Told by an idiot. . .Signifying nothing'. Nothing exists but illusion, the theatrical pretence of the 'poor player' – or, as he had put it when his imagination was first mastered by the Witches' illusory promises for the future, 'Nothing is But what is not' (see page 12). That has become his settled attitude.

3.2 EVIL

The idea of evil as negation and illusion is given convincing expression in *Macbeth*. For orthodox Christianity evil must be essentially negative. God created the whole universe; all reality is therefore good, and evil can only be unreality, a denial of that creation. It is inevitably destructive, and also self-destructive. Shakespeare's achievement is to bring this home imaginatively to audiences who do not necessarily share these theological beliefs; we are made to experience the psychological aridity involved in murder. Macbeth expresses the same theological principle in relation to God's hierarchical ordering of the universe (see pages 4-5) when he protests,

> I dare do all that may become a man;
> Who dares do more is none. (I.vii.46–7)

Man *is* man because he occupies that particular rank in creation. If he tries to rise above that rank he is merely denying his own nature and becomes 'none'; at best he can only sink to a lower rank, and Lady Macbeth is theologically correct in suggesting that he must therefore have been a beast when he originally suggested the murder of Duncan (I.vii.47–8). His crimes become increasingly bestial, and at the end of the play his courage is that of a cornered animal: 'bear-like I must fight the course' (V.vii.2).

By murdering Duncan he is destroying himself. His 'single state of man' had been shaken by his inner conflict, and the progressive disintegration of his personality is symbolised by the repeated opposition between his hands and his eyes. He can steel himself to murder only by repressing everything that gives him worth as a human being, so that he 'Moves like a ghost' (II.i.56), and his repressed feelings strike back violently with the hallucination of the dagger and the uncontrollable self-accusations under which he disintegrates completely after the murder. He is totally alienated from himself: 'To know my deed, 'twere best not know myself' (II.ii.73). He recovers an appearance of composure but he is still at war with himself; his moral feelings are no longer under his control because he has expelled them from his consciousness, and they continue to torment him in his dreams and with the ghost of Banquo that forces him actually to betray himself. However rigorously he represses it, his self-condemnation is implanted deeply in his mind; as Menteith says,

> Who then shall blame
> His pestered senses to recoil and start,

When all that is within him does condemn
Itself for being there? (V.ii.22-5)

For most of the last three acts of the play Macbeth is in a highly neurotic state, alternating between black melancholy and outbursts of 'valiant fury' that are akin to madness (V.ii.13-14) and lead him into totally irrational actions such as the massacre of Macduff's family and the suicidal act of abandoning the defences of Dunsinane castle.

As evil is essentially negative it must work through illusions to conceal its real nature. The Witches personify that nature; just as the forms taken by the Apparitions reveal the true meaning of their words (see page 38), so the Witches and their charms symbolise the chaotic, arid spiritual state to which Macbeth and Lady Macbeth will be reduced, but they conceal this by offering illusions, the illusion of kingship without true royalty and of security that turns out to be a source of insecurity (see pages 50 and 52). Evil must equivocate, and it forces its victims to equivocate with themselves. Having seen the reality of himself immediately after he has murdered Duncan, Macbeth can only cling to illusions as he relies desperately on the equivocations of the Apparitions as an assurance of his safety. Not only does he discover that the temporary disguise he had adopted to conceal his designs against Duncan must become a permanent mask (see page 32), but when that fails he must delude himself into thinking that his disturbed state of mind is caused only by fear and that the assaults of his repressed conscience are a 'self-abuse' that will be cured by even more heinous crimes (III.iv.141-2). In moods of elation he can refer to himself as 'our high-placed Macbeth' (IV.i.98) or tell his wife to be 'jocund' when another murder is planned (III.ii.40), but when he pauses to think he knows the hollowness of this bravado, and his barbarous crimes are less a way to ensure his safety than to escape from 'the torture of the mind' on which he continues 'to lie In restless ecstasy' (III.ii.21-2).

He flies from thought into mindless action, from the dispiriting chill of words to the 'heat of deeds' (II.i.61), and his actions become increasingly impetuous to avoid the agony of thinking: 'This deed I'll do before this purpose cool' (IV.i.144-54). But when he is trapped in Dunsinane castle all his feverish activity – hanging out banners, skirring the country round, arming before it is necessary – cannot prevent him from lapsing into those periods of desolate reflection that show his awareness of his actual situation. We may admire his refusal to submit passively to defeat – some critics have compared it to Satan's heroic defiance of God in *Paradise Lost* – but our sympathy for him springs primarily from a realisation that he is still haunted by the values that he consciously renounced, and his despair at their loss gives them a reality that makes the admirable piety of Malcolm seem somewhat complacent.

4 DRAMATIC TECHNIQUES

4.1 SHAKESPEARE'S USE OF HIS SOURCE

Shakespeare took the plot of *Macbeth* from Holinshed's *Chronicles of England, Scotland and Ireland* (1577). It was already a dramatic narrative, with a number of details that grew in his imagination to become major themes in the play. The prophecies of the Witches were part of the original story, and the second set of predictions already had that equivocal nature that Shakespeare was to develop as the all-pervading characteristic of evil in *Macbeth*; his witches, however, owe little to Holinshed's 'weird sisters' other than their prophetic words (see pages 6-7), and the Cauldron Scene with its Apparitions was his own invention. For the characterisation the *Chronicles* provided, at most, only preliminary sketches. The complex character of Macbeth is developed from the statement that

> the pricke of conscience. . .caused him ever to feare, least he should be served of the same cup, as he had ministred to his predecessor

- which also provided one seminal image for the play (I.vii.10-12). The role of Lady Macbeth is almost entirely Shakespeare's addition. Holinshed says that she encouraged her husband, and some further suggestions for her development may have come from another episode in the *Chronicles*: the murder of King Duff by Donwald, captain of the castle of Forres. Donwald's wife kindled his wrath, advised him to take advantage of Duff's great trust in him by committing the murder while he lodged unguarded in the castle, and 'shewed him the meanes wherby he might soonest accomplish it'. Having made Duff's two chamberlains drunk at a banquet, Donwald had Duff murdered, 'though he abhorred the act greatlie in heart', and when the bed was discovered 'all beraied with bloud' made a great display of innocence and slew the chamberlains 'as guiltie of that heinous murther'. This blood-stained bed may have made some contribution to the horror of the murder in the play, while the voice that Macbeth heard crying 'Sleep no more!' may have been suggested by Holinshed's account of the pangs of guilt suffered by another Scottish king, Kenneth, whose sleep was disturbed by a voice threatening him with vengeance for the murder of his nephew.

While Shakespeare developed the characters, he considerably simplified the political situation described by Holinshed so that the play focuses on their inner lives and on the moral implications of their actions. In the *Chronicles* Banquo is an accomplice in the murder of Duncan and is not murdered himself until ten years later. Macbeth has some justification for seizing the throne; he was next in line until Malcolm came of age, and by prematurely creating his son Prince of Cumberland Duncan was trying to exclude Macbeth from the succession. Moreover, while Duncan was 'soft and gentle of nature' he 'had too much of clemencie' and was negligent in punishing offenders, so that Macbeth's stern but just rule was initially welcomed. With these moral complications eliminated the play becomes a much more concentrated study of evil.

The concentration is increased by the telescoping of the historical events. The three campaigns that Macbeth fought against Macdonald, Sweno and a Danish army are abbreviated by omitting the third and reporting the first two in a single short scene as if they were an almost continuous action. Macbeth reigned for seventeen years, but his ten years of just rule are omitted and the extended period of tyranny is represented by the murder of Macduff's family and the general reports of atrocities. The commentary on the Banquet Scene has pointed out how our perception is manipulated so that while we gain a general impression of time having passed events seem to follow hard upon each other, increasing the sense of inevitability by the speed with which retribution follows sin.

4.2 STRUCTURE

Macbeth is the shortest of Shakespeare's tragedies and the most rapid in its movement. It has no subplot, and the main events of its single unified action are highlighted to leave less important matters undefined in the shadows. We do not know when, or if, Macbeth originally proposed the murder of Duncan (I.vii.47–52), why a third murderer appears (III.iii), or how Macduff weighed his responsibility to Scotland against that to his family, but an audience would gain a general impression of Macbeth's evil inclinations before he met the Witches, of a tyrant's inability to trust his own agents, and of the moral dilemmas tyranny creates for honest men; it would not have time to worry about the detailed circumstances.

The formal structure of the action also reinforces its moral theme, suggesting the exact balance of the retribution against the crime by 'even-handed justice' (I.vii.10). It is organised symmetrically about the Banquet Scene. The first half of the play shows Macbeth's rise to power, the second his fall, the two movements being interrelated by the murder of Banquo. This murder that was intended to ensure Macbeth's safety actually leads to his exposure and his overthrow. Shakespeare's tragedies often begin with a scene that presents, not the major characters, but the underlying forces that will determine the action. In *Macbeth* the parallelism of the two halves is emphasised by prefacing both with the Witches, who prompt the action that is to follow and give outward expression to the evil already working in Macbeth's mind; and their two prophetic scenes are also parallel to each other, in each three statements about Macbeth are followed by the prediction of Banquo's royal line. The formality of the structure is increased by the complementary development of the characters of Macbeth and Lady Macbeth: while he becomes more hardened in evil she weakens, until in the end she finds his earlier fears being realised in her dreams while he is priding himself on the callousness that she exulted in at the beginning.

This deliberate structuring of the play to draw attention to its moral theme is reminiscent of the morality plays that were still being performed at the end of the sixteenth century. They dramatised the conflict between good and evil in the soul of man. The central character represented humanity in general – he is given names such as 'Everyman' or 'Mankind' – and the other characters were personifications of virtues and vices, or angels and devils, which acted out a moral allegory. The role of the Witches in *Macbeth* resembles that of the morality devils, and there are several references to morality characters: Lady Macbeth refers to a 'painted devil' (II.ii.55), and Macbeth likens himself to a personified 'withered Murder' (II.i.52). The 'devil-porter' of Hell was a familiar, often comic, character in these plays; the Porter is in effect improvising a scene from a morality in which 'hell-mouth' would have been represented physically on the stage. His satirical comedy links *Macbeth* to this tradition of explicitly moral drama.

There are several scenes which serve to provide a more general moral context for the central action of the play, such as those between Ross and the Old Man and between Lennox and a Lord, in which the characters, performing a similar function to that of the chorus in Greek tragedy, stand back from the action and make clear its universal implications – showing how

the heavens, as troubled with man's act,
Threaten his bloody stage (II.iv.5–6)

and invoking the aid of 'Some holy angel' to 'Fly to the court of England' (III.vi.45–6). The scene in England has a similar function in presenting a generalised image of tyranny and contrasting with it the ideal of the true king, personified in the saintly figure of Edward the Confessor (see pages 41–2).

These scenes are relatively flat compared with those that show the live interaction of characters, and have an orderly structure that suits their plain didactic purpose – although even III.vi is enlivened by the irony of Lennox, and the temper of IV.iii changes dramatically, of course, with the entrance of Ross. Shakespeare, in fact, was sometimes content to use second-hand material for these background scenes: Malcolm's testing of Macduff is largely a paraphrase of Holinshed's account, and the portents described in II.iv reproduce those that followed the murder of King Duff.

4.3 SECONDARY CHARACTERS

The characters who appear in these scenes are also relatively flat; they are given the attributes necessary for their representative role in the play. In addition to serving frequently as a messenger, Ross represents the general attitudes of the Scottish nobility in his distress at the murder of Duncan and his initial acceptance of Macbeth's accession, and only acquires some individuality with his sympathy for Lady Macduff and her son and his anguished reporting of their murder to Macduff. Lennox has a more personal voice in the irony of his farewell at the end of the banquet (III.iv. 119-20) and of his long speech in III.vi, but even that has a representative function in setting out in an orderly manner Macbeth's various crimes, to which the eyes of the nobles have now been opened. And this emergence of Lennox as a personality does not prevent his use as an apparently loyal attendant on Macbeth in IV.i (see page 37).

Malcolm is a major actor in the drama, but his characterisation is clearly determined by the need to make him the antithesis of Macbeth – in his orderly conduct of affairs, his piety, his combination of resolution with prudence, and his youth. This last attribute is conveyed more dramatically, perhaps, by his clumsy effort to comfort Macduff and his youthful optimism about the outcome of the battle, but while we may admire Malcolm it is doubtful if we know him sufficiently as an individual to sympathise greatly with him – except, perhaps, at that moment of vulnerable isolation expressed by his covert interchange with Donalbain after the murder of their father (II.iii.118-23, 133-44). Macduff has a similar role in the pattern of the play as the champion of legitimate monarchy, but the vehemence of his horror on discovering the murdered King, his blunt refusal to temporise with Macbeth – 'with an absolute "Sir, not I"' (III.vi.40) – and his stunned grief when he learns of the massacre of his family give substance to his character. His exposure of them to Macbeth's vengeance is a genuine issue in the play, made more real by the distress of Lady Macduff. The conflict between her sense of betrayal and loyalty to her husband and the sad playfulness of her conversation with her son make her also one of the more individual of the secondary characters.

But the only character developed sufficiently to contrast with Macbeth as much by what he is as by what he says and does is Banquo. His role was determined by the contrast between the fertility of his royal progeny and the sterility of Macbeth's reign, but Shakespeare's imagination has worked on this idea. The imagery of natural fertility that gathers about him (see pages 13 and 17) – suggested initially by the Witches' prophecy – conveys also a sense of his magnanimity, a generosity of character that leads him to ignore the implications of Macbeth's crafty questioning about his movements on the day of his murder; such low cunning is entirely alien to his frank nature (see pages 12-13 and 29). As Macbeth's dark, tormented soul is projected outwards into the imagery of night, so Banquo's equable temperament is reflected in the tranquil atmosphere of his description of the martlets (I.vi.3-10). Thus by the time we hear Macbeth's tribute to his 'royalty of nature' (III.i.49) he is only expressing what we have already felt about him. In consequence his failure to act against Macbeth is a problem that cannot be avoided (see page 29), but his character has a complexity that leaves it open to various interpretations. Compared with the unambiguous but inert virtues of Malcolm he has the vitality of real life.

The limited development of most of the secondary characters focuses attention on Macbeth and Lady Macbeth. Their characters, and the moral drama played out in their minds, are examined in detail throughout the Critical Commentary and in Themes and Issues.

4.4 IMAGERY AND IRONY

The internal action within the minds of the principal characters is most powerfully conveyed through imagery, for it is through images and dreams that one penetrates into the deeper recesses of the mind, as in Lady Macbeth's sleep-walking, in Macbeth's soliloquy that begins I.vii and in the scenes that follow the murders of Duncan and Banquo. The intricate and closely-knit pattern of imagery, which has already been examined in detail in the Critical Commentary, gives the play its remarkable imaginative unity. As well as taking us inside the minds of the characters it establishes the mood of the play, dominated by blood and darkness, and embodies its themes, giving them vivid concrete expression: the blood coagulates on the murderers' hands, the darkness they summon enters their souls – 'hell is murky'.

The imagery is the source of much of the dramatic irony of the play – irony that arises when a character is not aware of the real, or full, significance of his words. The audience sometimes recognises it at the time – they will know, for example, that Duncan's comment on the treachery of the Thane of Cawdor (I.iv.11–14) is likely to be applicable to the new Cawdor as well as to the old – but sometimes it does not emerge until later, when it may also be made clear to the speaker. It is particularly common in *Macbeth* since the general theme of the play is the discovery by Macbeth and Lady Macbeth of the real significance of their words, thoughts and actions. Individual words and images, often introduced casually, reverberate through the play, sometimes gaining more significance, sometimes changing it – as the meaning of the word 'done' is subtly changed to express their realisation that they will never escape from their crimes (see page 57). Lady Macbeth refers cynically to the ruthlessness her husband lacks as an 'illness' (I.v.19), and the unintentional appropriateness of the term appears later in the actual psychological disorders that afflict them both. This metaphor is an apt expression of the principle that one's actions are not external to oneself but are absorbed into one's system, and this is brought home in simple concrete terms by its connection with the two basic requirements for health, sleep and food, which are often associated in the play (II.ii.37–40, III.ii.17–19, iv.140, vi.34–5).

Moreover, as these metaphors develop they are often represented in literal form on the stage. Duncan first introduces the metaphor of feasting when he describes the praise of Macbeth's loyal service as a 'banquet' to him (I.iv.56), and one major consequence of Macbeth's treachery is represented symbolically by his isolation from the two actual banquets. This symbol pervades the play in both metaphorical and literal form, and often with ironic effect. Macbeth sees his crime metaphorically as a 'poisoned chalice' (I.vii.11) and his fear that it will be commended to his own lips is realised when it is his act, literally, of drinking a health to Banquo that prompts the entry of the ghost to force him to reveal his guilt; Lady Macbeth uses 'wine and wassail' literally to drug the grooms (I.vii.64) and as a result of their violation of the laws of hospitality Macbeth discovers that, metaphorically, 'The wine of life is drawn' (II.iii.93); even the Witches' 'hell-broth', their 'gruel' (IV.i.19,32), is a satanic inversion of the potent symbol of the banquet. Similarly the terrible images of infancy in Macbeth's vision of avenging innocence and Lady Macbeth's demonstration of her ruthlessness (I.vii.21–2, 54–8) rise from the cauldron in the forms of the Second and Third Apparitions, which prove to be heralds of vengeance when Macbeth finds they have betrayed him; the metaphors of youth, fertility and resurgent nature associated with Banquo, Malcolm and Macduff's son are literally represented by the youth of Malcolm's army; the apparition of the crowned child has a tree in his hand, and when Birnam wood is seen to be advancing on Dunsinane nature itself seems to be rising against Macbeth. Poetic metaphor and dramatic action are intertwined, giving the play its peculiarly dense imaginative texture; this is 'poetic drama' with neither the poetry nor the drama subordinated to the other.

Shakespeare's ability to think concretely, through metaphor, makes the expression still more compressed; a single image can convey a wealth of meaning and subtle nuances of feeling. Sometimes the verse lingers meditatively over an idea, expanding it through an organised series of images (V.v.19-28); sometimes the thought moves so rapidly from one image to the next that the first is overlaid by the second – as the idea of spurring a horse is overtaken by that of vaulting, and 'heaven's cherubim' riding the winds, 'the sightless couriers of the air', merge into the winds themselves and 'blow the horrid deed in every eye' (I.vii.25-8, 22-4). The movement of the imagery catches the swift intuitive movement of the mind.

4.5 VERSE AND PROSE

As in all Shakespeare's later plays, the blank verse adapts flexibly to the dramatic expression. The orderly progression of Malcolm's speeches in IV.iii is quite different from the congested movement of the verse when Macbeth wrestles with the idea of murder (I.iii.137-42, vii.1-7), and that again differs from the more expansive rhythm with which he concludes his general reflections on the worthlessness of life (V.v.23-8) – the whole speech is analysed in detail on pages 69-72 to show how subtle changes in mood are expressed by inconspicuous changes in verse movement. There is a wide range of verse style in the play: at one extreme is the supple intricacy of Macbeth's and Lady Macbeth's courtly speeches (I.iv.22-7, vi.14-20, 25-8) and the equally elaborate but broader and more flamboyant verse of the Captain (I.ii); at the other, the broken verse of Macbeth and his wife immediately after the murder of Duncan (II.ii.16-20) and of Macduff after he hears of the murder of his family (IV.iii.211-17), but while the former has a tense nervousness Macduff's grief-striken phrases each fall dead and flat.

Shakespeare's prose is equally flexible and expressive, and is certainly not reserved – as is sometimes said – for lower-class characters and less dramatic episodes. In *Macbeth* each passage of prose has a highly distinctive character: there is the polished fluency of Macbeth's letter; the Porter's earthy wit; the domestic intimacy of Lady Macduff and her son; and the fragmented intensity of Lady Macbeth's sleep-walking.

Macbeth also has – for the tragedies – a high proportion of rhymed verse. That of the Witches has already been discussed (page 9), and there are numerous rhymed couplets elsewhere in the play. These sometimes have the practical function of indicating the end of a scene, but some occur earlier in the scene, such as the pair of couplets that seem to link

Macbeth's invocation to night with the incantation of the Witches (I.iv. 50-3) and those that sum up Lady Macbeth's disillusionment,

> Nought's had, all's spent,
> Where our desire is got without content.
> 'Tis safer to be that which we destroy
> Than by destruction dwell in doubtful joy. (III.ii.4-7)

They are often used, like those just quoted, to highlight important themes in the play –

> But hold thee still,
> Things bad begun make strong themselves by ill. (III.ii.54-5)

In contrast to the flexible blank verse that adapts to the individual expression of each character they punctuate the dramatic action with neat proverbial statements that focus sharply on the general moral issues which emerge from the play's exploration of the experience of two individual murderers.

5 SPECIMEN CRITICAL ANALYSIS

A cry of women within

MACBETH   What is that noise?

SEYTON   It is the cry of women, my good lord.   *Exit*

MACBETH   I have almost forgot the taste of fears.
    The time has been my senses would have cooled   10
    To hear a night-shriek, and my fell of hair
    Would at a dismal treatise rouse and stir
    As life were in't. I have supped full with horrors;
    Direness, familiar to my slaughterous thoughts,
    Cannot once start me.   *Enter* SEYTON
              Wherefore was that cry?

SEYTON   The Queen, my lord, is dead.

MACBETH   She should have died hereafter;
    There would have been a time for such a word.
    Tomorrow, and tomorrow, and tomorrow,
    Creeps in this petty pace from day to day,   20
    To the last syllable of recorded time;
    An all our yesterdays have lighted fools
    The way to dusty death. Out, out, brief candle!
    Life's but a walking shadow, a poor player
    That struts and frets his hour upon the stage
    And then is heard no more. It is a tale
    Told by an idiot, full of sound and fury,
    Signifying nothing.   (V.v.7-28)

Macbeth is flinging defiance at his enemies when he is interrupted by a
wailing cry. It is an eerie sound, linked by his reference to a 'night-shriek'
to the similar sounds heard while he was murdering Duncan – the owl's cry
that startled even Lady Macbeth – but there is no weaking of his resolution.

The speech that follows might even be continuing his earlier bravado, but he is not exulting in the fact that he has 'almost forgot the taste of fears'; the rhythm is too steady and controlled for that, and 'almost' shows the restraint with which he considers the contrast between his past and present states of mind. As he relives his earlier highly-strung reactions the language is very sensory: he recalls the 'taste' of fear – perhaps the dry palate that prevented his saying 'Amen' – and the sudden chill when his 'senses would have cooled'; he feels the thickness of his 'fell' of hair 'rouse and stir', with surprise at its unnaturalness, 'As life were in't' – the two verbs show the precision with which the experience is being recalled, and one remembers how the thought of murder 'unfixed' his hair after he met the Witches.

As the 'night-shriek' recalls the murder of Duncan, 'supped full with horrors' recalls that of Banquo, when the horror of Banquo's ghost replaced the conviviality of the banquet. One reads 'supped. . .with' as 'supped . . .on' and this is its primary meaning, but 'supped. . .with' is also appropriate: he has both metaphorically feasted on horrors and feasted with them as he has eaten his 'meal in fear'. Similarly the primary meaning of 'familiar to' is that he is accustomed to 'Direness' – horror – but there may also be a suggestion of the witch's familiar; as it prompts the malign actions of the witch, so the horror with which Macbeth has to live drives him to further slaughter – his demon is the horror he has himself created in his own mind. At the end of the Banquet Scene he concluded that his panic was 'the initiate fear that wants hard use'; this speech shows the extent to which a familiarity with horror has inured him to it, and the deliberate movement of the last sentence, with the accent falling heavily on 'Direness' and the savage 'slaughterous thoughts', has a sinister calm that reflects the cold-bloodedness he describes.

The calm continues as Macbeth turns abruptly to Seyton. This is a climactic moment in the play, but Lady Macbeth's death excites no emotional outburst. Seyton's brief, factual statement need not imply indifference, it might be tinged with awe, but Macbeth does not seem greatly moved; he does not even ask how she died. One might conclude that he has lost all regard for her, especially if the next sentence means that she should have died later, when he would have had leisure to attend to the news. But as the rest of the speech implies that it would have made no difference when she died, it is more likely to be expressing a bleak fatalism – she would have died in the future anyway, the word of her death would have arrived at some time or another. This dismisses Lady Macbeth less callously, and the speech as a whole shows that if Macbeth no longer values his wife it is because the whole of life has lost its value; indeed, it is the news of her death that brings home to him the pointlessness of living.

The lines that follow are weighed down with a sense of life's futility by the dragging repetition of 'Tomorrow, and tomorrow, and tomorrow'.

These 'tomorrow's are balanced by 'all our yesterdays' to encompass the full extent of 'recorded time', which is reduced to a meaningless succession of undifferentiated days; the record of time is broken down into meaningless 'syllables'. Daylight has guided men only to death; 'fools' embraces the whole of mankind, foolish in not realising that that is all they will achieve. Macbeth is concerned with nothing beyond this life: his survey stops with 'the last syllable of recorded time', and 'dusty death' has no supernatural terrors, only an arid triviality. The rhythm of these lines itself 'Creeps' tediously through the drawn-out pauses of line 19 and the halting monosyllables and the trivial alliteration of 'petty pace' in line 20, until it almost comes to a halt after 'recorded time'.

From this point there is an imaginative quickening as Macbeth becomes immersed in his vision of the worthlessness of life. The rhythm becomes rather more fluent and is given further impetus by the impatience of 'Out, out, brief candle!'; the momentum increases as the images accumulate. The subject of each of the three parallel statements with which the speech concludes is the initial word 'Life', giving the lines more continuity: 'Life's but a walking shadow' is picked up by 'a poor player', and the rhythm moves easily over the enjambment to the pause at the end of the sentence, where it receives new energy from the alliteration as it swings over the end of the line - 'It is a tale/Told' - before concluding with the finality of 'Signifying nothing', stopping emphatically in the middle of the line.

The imagery is also subtly interwoven. The 'candle', a precarious form of illumination, is suggested by 'lighted fools' in the previous line, and in turn suggests the shadow of the person walking by the light of the candle - there is no other reason for introducing 'walking' as it is the 'shadow' that expresses the insubstantial nature of life. The 'poor player' - an actor - follows from 'shadow', for actors were often described as shadows, presenting only a phantom illusion of reality. With a magnificent gesture, Shakespeare suddenly brings the performance of his own play into the imagery as a symbol of the unreality of life, reminding his audience that they are participating in just such an illusory experience that will cease to exist once the actors have left the stage. 'Struts and frets' relates Macbeth's disillusioned view of all human activity both to his own strutting and fretting within the castle of Dunsinane and to the heightened action and speech of the actor who plays him on the stage of the Globe. The imagery increases in intensity from the insubstantial 'shadow' to the pathetic 'player' and then to the outright absurdity of 'an idiot', while the neutral 'walking' changes to the trivial self-importance of 'struts and frets', heightened by the clipped alliteration, and finally to the tumult of 'sound and fury', before the sudden anticlimax, 'Signifying nothing'.

When Macbeth was hailed as 'King hereafter' he expressed his delighted anticipation in the imagery of the stage:

> Two truths are told
> As happy prologues to the swelling act
> Of the imperial theme;

this speech shows that he now understands the full implications of the metaphor. It expands on his earlier description of life as a 'fitful fever', in contrast to which the peace of death enjoyed by Duncan is greatly to be preferred; it is perhaps appropriate then as the only epitaph that Lady Macbeth gets.

6 CRITICAL APPROACHES

Macbeth has always been one of Shakespeare's most popular plays. From 1674 it was performed in the adaptation by Sir William D'Avenant, who altered it radically to suit the taste of the time, but in 1744 Garrick largely restored the original text for his own performances as Macbeth. There are few critical comments on the play from before this time, and the greatest critic of the eighteenth century, Dr Johnson, was not at his best on *Macbeth*. He approved of its morality, as he interpreted it –

> The passions are directed to their true end. Lady Macbeth is merely detested; and though the courage of Macbeth preserves some esteem, yet every reader rejoices in his fall –

but considered that 'it has no nice discriminations of character' and that some of the language – daggers 'breeched' [put into breeches] with gore; heaven peeping through a blanket – was too low for the dignity of its subject. He provoked, however, the first detailed critical study of the imagery of the play, Walter Whiter's *Specimen of a Commentary on Shakespeare* (1794). Developing some suggestions from the Shakespeare scholar, Edward Malone – for example, that the 'blanket' was the thick curtain of the Jacobean stage – Whiter showed the interrelation of the numerous 'theatrical' images in the play, and linked them with the imagery of darkness and hell by referring to the Jacobean practice of draping the stage in black for the performance of tragedy and to the numerous references to 'Hell-mouth' as one of the stage propeties owned by acting companies.

Another relatively early inquiry into the imaginative impact of the play is Thomas De Quincey's essay 'On the Knocking on the Gate in *Macbeth*' (1823). He explores the powerful effect the knocking had always had on him by comparing the situation in the play to that in real life when ordinary activities have been temporarily suspended – at a state funeral, for example; he points out that we are most aware of this suspension – the unnatural silence of the city – when we hear ordinary life resuming – 'the sound of wheels rattling away from the scene'. Similarly, the knocking on the gate indicates 'the re-establishment of the goings-on of the world', and draws our attention to the suspension of normal life that has preceded it, with Macbeth and Lady Macbeth 'taken out of the region of human things' and 'conformed to the image of devils'.

Nineteenth century critics, however, were chiefly concerned with the characters in the play, an approach that culminated in A. C. Bradley's *Shakespearean Tragedy* (1904). Its value can be illustrated by comparing Johnson's blanket dismissal of Macbeth and his wife with Bradley's characteristic insights:

> the deed [the murder of Duncan] is done in horror and without the faintest desire or sense of glory – done, one may almost say, as if it were an appalling duty;

the lines in which Lady Macbeth explains why she does not kill Duncan herself (II.ii.12–13) are probably spoken

> without any sentiment – impatiently, as though she regretted her weakness: but it was there.

Bradley also surveys the imagery to show how it contributes to the atmosphere of the play, and examines the dramatic structure in broad terms, pointing out, for example, the problem of maintaining interest in Act IV after the initial action has reached its climax and before the counter-action has gathered momentum – a problem that is solved in *Macbeth* by introducing the excitement of the Cauldron Scene and the pathos of Lady Macduff and her son.

The danger of concentrating on character to the neglect of other components of a play is that the characters come to be thought of as real people rather than as characters in a play, a weakness that was amusingly parodied in the title of L. C. Knights's essay 'How Many Children Had Lady Macbeth?' (1933, published in *Explorations*, 1946) – how Lady Macbeth could have 'given suck' (I.vii.54) when the Macbeths are childless is, of course, only a problem if one tries to construct a biography for her outside the confines of the play. For Knights, *Macbeth* is a dramatic poem, to be valued not merely for the 'realism' of the characters, but because character, action and imagery all contribute to its central themes – the reversal of values, unnatural disasters and deceitful appearance. Scenes that had been dismissed as unrealistic or tedious are shown to be organically related to these themes: I.ii is 'full of images of confusion'; in his self-accusations in IV.iii Malcolm 'has ceased to be a person' and is acting instead 'as a mirror wherein the ills of Scotland are reflected'.

Without too much over-simplification one might date the modern practice of closely analysing the poetic character of Shakespeare's plays from the early 1930s. In *The Imperial Theme* (1931) G. Wilson Knight interpreted *Macbeth* as a symbolic pattern of 'life-themes' – 'Warrior-honour', 'Imperial magnificence', 'Sleep and Feasting' and 'Ideas of creation and nature's innocence'. At times these themes seem to be assuming as autonomous an existence as that of the 'characters' in nineteenth-century criticism, but they lead to many valuable insights – for example, on Macbeth's comparison of himself to Tarquin (II.i.55): 'Macbeth's evil is a lust, like unruly love; a centring of reality in the self'. In 1935 Caroline Spurgeon's *Shakespeare's Imagery and What it Tells Us* directed attention specifically to the image groupings in the plays, and with more regard for their dramatic structure. She was the first, for example, to point out the significance of the imagery of borrowed clothes in *Macbeth* (see page 46):

> This imaginative picture of a small ignoble man encumbered and degraded by garments unsuited to him should be put against the view emphasised by some critics of the likeness between Macbeth and Milton's Satan in grandeur and sublimity.

Later critics have continued to explore the imaginative nature of the play. In *The Well-Wrought Urn* (1947) Cleanth Brooks related Miss Spurgeon's clothing images to the imagery of concealment and deception – including the daggers 'breeched with gore' that offended Dr. Johnson – and examined the significance of the imagery of childhood. In *Shakespeare's Wordplay* (1957) M. M. Mahood analysed the subtle expressiveness of Shakespeare's puns and *doubles entendres* – when Macduff summons Malcolm and Banquo to 'countenance this horror' (II.iii.79) 'countenance' means for him 'be in keeping with', but

> it also means for Shakespeare. . . 'give tacit consent to'. By a time-serving assent to Macbeth's election, Banquo puts himself in a position of danger and finally is murdered.

This increasingly detailed study of the text has been complemented by the historical inquiries of other critics. Johnson had provided lengthy notes on witchcraft for the benefit of the more sceptical eighteenth-century reader and audience, and the subsequent growth of historical awareness has shown the need to understand a play in the context of its own time. In *Shakespeare's Philosophical Patterns* (1937) W. O. Curry set out the medieval ways of thought that still permeated the outlook of the Elizabethans, and in *The Royal Play of Macbeth* (1948) H. N. Paul has made a fascinating study of the immediate circumstances of the writing of the play.

There is a wealth of recent criticism to assist a student in interpreting *Macbeth*, but its relevance needs to be carefully assessed. There is clearly a risk of excessive ingenuity in interpreting the minutiae of the text, and it is equally misleading to assume that Shakespeare's outlook was inevitably 'cabined, cribbed, confined' by the received opinions of his own age – as Ben Jonson wrote, he was not of an age, but for all time – or that he incorporated anything into the play *merely* for its topical interest. *Macbeth* is probably the most unified of Shakespeare's plays, and the value of different critical opinions must be continually tested against the total impression it creates.

QUESTIONS

These questions are intended to help you to explore the play further, either by discussing them with other people, thinking about them yourself, or writing answers – you often do not realise how much you have to say about a subject until you start to write. Most of them can be answered at very different levels, but the important thing is to support your opinions by precise reference to the play, and to consider all the aspects of it that are relevant to the question.

1. Which do you think were more influential in persuading Macbeth to murder Duncan, the Witches or Lady Macbeth?

2. 'The historical Macbeth thought he had some claim to the throne; by ignoring this in the play Shakespeare made the moral issues much too simple – people are not merely "good" or "bad".' How would you reply to this criticism?

3. Is Lady Macbeth primarily moved by love for her husband and an unselfish wish to help him gain the throne, or does she merely use him as an instrument by which to realise her own ambition?

4. 'Malcolm's callous remark ['this dead butcher'] shocks us into a recognition of Macbeth's potential greatness – a greatness that can endure solitude'; Lady Macbeth 'was too great to repent'. Does one continue to admire Macbeth or Lady Macbeth in the last three acts?

5. Do you find that you are sympathising more with Malcolm or with Macbeth at the end of the play? Consider the reasons for your response.

6. Write an additional scene for the play (it does not *have* to be in blank verse) in which
   either Macbeth and Lady Macbeth consider the murder of Duncan before he meets the Witches, as she implies they had done (I.vii.47–52) – you need not assume that her account of it is entirely accurate,

78

although it could not be totally false; *or* Banquo, Lennox, Ross and Macduff discuss the murder of Duncan – 'question this most bloody piece of work' (II.iii.126) – and consider the likely accession of Macbeth to the throne.

7. Why do *you* think Banquo failed to oppose Macbeth's accession? Everything he says and does in the play *might* be relevant.

8. Consider how far you agree with the statement on page 64 that the secondary characters are relatively flat. Decide which of them might be made most interesting as an individual and describe how you would present him or her on the stage, either as actor or producer.

9. By what different means does Shakespeare produce a feeling of suspense in either the characters or the audience?

10. Does the excitement of the play depend more on Shakespeare's surprising the audience by the turn of events or by letting them know in advance what is going to happen?

11. Shakespeare could not assume his audience would know the story of Macbeth. By what different means does he give them the information they need?

12. Examine all the uses of the word 'nature' (including related words such as 'natural' and 'unnatural') in the play in order to explain as precisely as possible what it means and its significance for the themes of the play.

13. In what different ways is the opposition between appearance and reality presented in the play?

14. For the purpose of conveying the themes of the play, what would be the advantages and disadvantages of setting a production in (a) eleventh-century Scotland, (b) Jacobean England or (c) your own country in the second half of the twentieth-century?

15. Make a close critical analysis of III.iv.13–31 ('There's blood upon thy face. . .We'll hear ourselves again') or examine the imagery in this passage to show how it relates to the themes of the play.

16.   How at Bankside, a boy drowning kittens
            Winced at the business; whereupon his sister –
            Lady Macbeth aged seven – thrust 'em under,
                    Sombrely scornful.
                    (Kipling: *The Craftsman*)

Write an account of a familiar situation in which one can see some aspect of the play reflected.

APPENDIX:

SHAKESPEARE'S THEATRE

We should speak, as Murel Bradbrook reminds us, not of the Elizabethan stage but of Elizabethan stages. Plays of Shakespeare were acted on tour, in the halls of mansions, one at least in Gray's Inn, frequently at Court, and after 1609 at the Blackfriars, a small, roofed theatre for those who could afford the price. But even after his Company acquired the Blackfriars, we know of no play of his not acted (unless, rather improbably, *Troilus* is an exception) for the general public at the Globe, or before 1599 at its predecessor, The Theatre, which, since the Globe was constructed from the same timbers, must have resembled it. Describing the Globe, we can claim therefore to be describing, in an acceptable sense, Shakespeare's theatre, the physical structure his plays were designed to fit. Even in the few probably written for a first performance elsewhere, adaptability to that structure would be in his mind.

For the facilities of the Globe we have evidence from the drawing of the Swan theatre (based on a sketch made by a visitor to London about 1596) which depicts the interior of another public theatre; the builder's contract for the Fortune theatre, which in certain respects (fortunately including the dimensions and position of the stage) was to copy the Globe; indications in the dramatic texts; comments, like Ben Jonson's on the throne let down from above by machinery; and eye-witness testimony to the number of spectators (in round figures, 3000) accommodated in the auditorium.

In communicating with the audience, the actor was most favourably placed. Soliloquising at the centre of the front of the great platform, he was at the mid-point of the theatre, with no one among the spectators more than sixty feet away from him. That platform-stage (Figs I and II) was the most important feature for performance at the Globe. It had the audience – standing in the yard (10) and seated in the galleries (9) – on three sides of it. It was 43 feet wide, and 27½ feet from front to back. Raised (?5½ feet) above the level of the yard, it had a trap-door (II.8)

SHAKESPEARE'S THEATRE

The stage and its adjuncts; the tiring-house; and the auditorium.

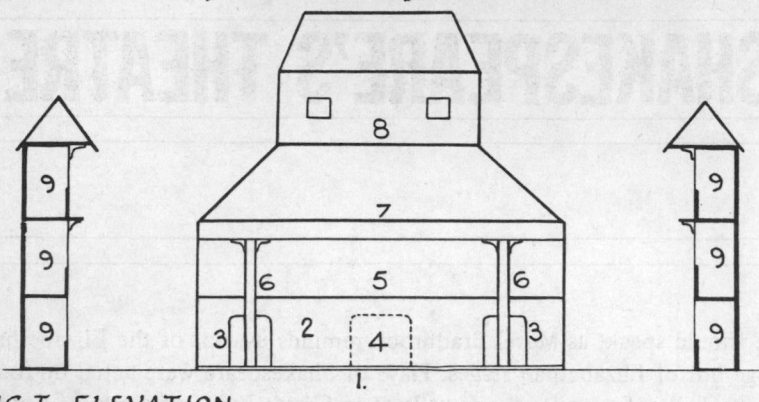

FIG I ELEVATION

1. Platform stage (approximately five feet above the ground) 2. Tiring-house
3. Tiring-house doors to stage 4. Conjectured third door 5. Tiring-house
gallery (balustrade and partitioning not shown) 6. Pillars supporting the
heavens 7. The heavens 8. The hut 9. The spectators' galleries

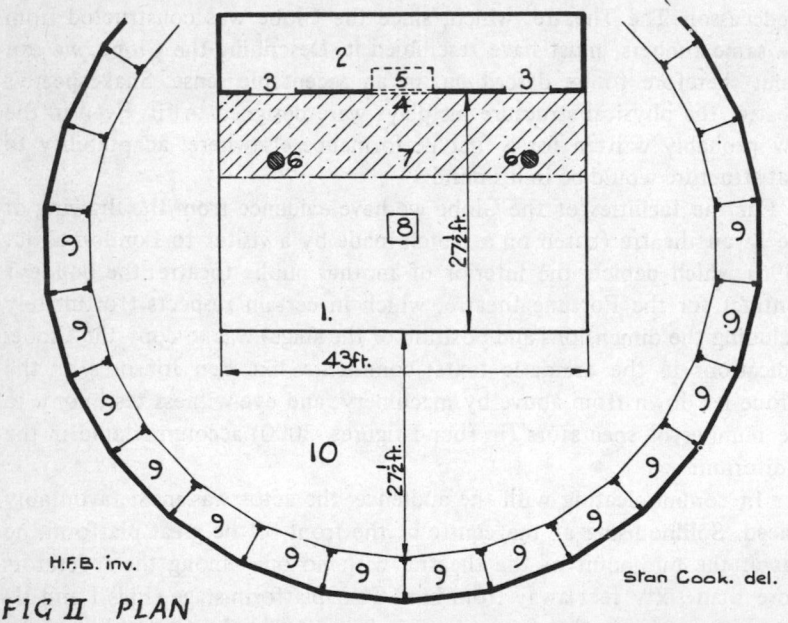

H.F.B. inv.

Stan Cook. del.

FIG II PLAN

1. Platform stage 2. Tiring-house 3. Tiring-house doors to stage
4. Conjectural third door 5. Conjectural discovery space (alternatively behind 3)
6. Pillars supporting the heavens 7. The heavens 8. Trap door 9. Spectators'
gallery 10. The yard

An artist's imaginative recreation of a typical Elizabethan theatre

giving access to the space below it. The actors, with their equipment, occupied the 'tiring house' (attiring-house: 2) immediately at the back of the stage. The stage-direction 'within' means inside the tiring-house. Along its frontage, probably from the top of the second storey, juts out the canopy or 'Heavens', carried on two large pillars rising through the platform (6, 7) and sheltering the rear part of the stage, the rest of which, like the yard, was open to the sky. If the 'hut' (I.8), housing the machinery for descents, stood, as in the Swan drawing, above the 'Heavens', that covering must have had a trap-door, so that the descents could be made through it.

Descents are one illustration of the vertical dimension the dramtist could use to supplement the playing-area of the great platform. The other opportunities are provided by the tiring-house frontage or facade. About this facade the evidence is not as complete or clear as we should like, so that Fig. I is in part conjectural. Two doors giving entry to the platform there certainly were (3). A third (4) is probable but not certain. When curtained, a door, most probably this one, would furnish what must be termed a discovery-space (II.5), not an inner stage (on which action in any depth would have been out of sight for a significant part of the audience). Usually no more than two actors were revealed (exceptionally, three), who often then moved out on to the platform. An example of this is Ferdinand and Miranda in *The Tempest* 'discovered' at chess, then seen on the platform speaking with their fathers. Similarly the gallery (I.5) was not an upper stage. Its use was not limited to the actors: sometimes it functioned as 'lords' rooms' for favoured spectators, sometimes, perhaps, as a musician's gallery. Frequently the whole gallery would not be needed for what took place aloft: a window-stage (as in the first balcony scene in *Romeo*, even perhaps in the second) would suffice. Most probably this would be a part (at one end) of the gallery itself; or just possibly, if the gallery did not (as it does in the Swan drawing) extend the whole width of the tiring-house, a window over the left or right-hand door. As the texts show, whatever was presented aloft, or in the discovery-space, was directly related to the action on the platform, so that at no time was there left, between the audience and the action of the drama, a great bare space of platform-stage. In relating Shakespeare's drama to the physical conditions of the theatre, the primacy of that platform is never to be forgotten.

Note: The present brief account owes most to C. Walter Hodges, *The Globe Restored*; Richard Hosley in *A New Companion to Shakespeare Studies*, and in *The Revels History of English Drama*; and to articles by Hosley and Richard Southern in *Shakespeare Survey*, 12, 1959, where full discussion can be found.

HAROLD BROOKS

FURTHER READING

Collections of Extracts from Important Critical Works
Hawkes, T. (ed.), *Twentieth Century Interpretations of Macbeth* (Prentice Hall, 1977)
Lerner, L. (ed.), *Shakespeare's Tragedies, an Anthology of Modern Criticism* (Penguin, 1963)
Wain, J. (ed.), *Macbeth, a Casebook* (Macmillan, 1968)

Critical Works Containing Substantial Sections on Macbeth
Bradley, A. C., *Shakespearean Tragedy* (Macmillan, 1904; paperback 1957)
Campbell, L. B., *Shakespeare's Tragic Heroes* (Cambridge University Press, 1930; paperback Methuen, 1961)
Holloway, J., *The Story of the Night* (Routledge & Kegan Paul, 1961)
Knight, G. Wilson, *The Imperial Theme* (revised ed. Methuen, 1951)
Knights, L. C., *Some Shakespearean Themes* (Chatto & Windus, 1959)
Mahood, M. M., *Shakespeare's Wordplay* (Methuen, 1957)
Muir, K. (ed.), *Shakespeare Survey 19* (Cambridge University Press, 1966)
Spurgeon, C., *Shakespeare's Imagery and What It Tells Us* (Cambridge University Press, 1935)
Walker, R., *The Time is Free* (Dakers, 1949)

The Contemporary Background of the Play
Paul, H. N., *The Royal Play of Macbeth* (Macmillan Company, New York, 1950)